mediterranean
GRILLING

More Than 100 Recipes
from Across the Mediterranean

DIANE KOCHILAS

WILLIAM MORROW

An Imprint of HarperCollinsPublishers

HarperCollins books may be purchased for educational, business, or sales promotional use. For information please write: Special Markets Department, HarperCollins Publishers, 10 East 53rd Street, New York, NY 10022.

FIRST EDITION

Photographs by Vassilis Stenos
Food styling by Tina Webb
Designed by Vertigo Design NYC

Library of Congress Cataloging-in-Publication Data has been applied for.

ISBN: 978-0-06-055639-6
ISBN-10: 0-06-055639-0

07 08 09 10 11 WBC/IM 10 9 8 7 6 5 4 3 2 1

FOR VASSILI, KYVELI, AND YIORGO, WITH ALL MY LOVE

CONTENTS

Books are always a team effort and working with good people is always one of the great pleasures of bringing a book to fruition. I have many people to thank.

Christos Valtsoglou, owner of Pylos, a rustic Greek restaurant in New York City's East Village, provides me with opportunity after opportunity to experiment with recipes and try them out on a willing clientele. Many of the dishes in this book were first grilled on the Pylos grill. Thanks! I also want to say thanks to Juan Tzitzimititla, the point man and kitchen expeditor at Pylos, who turns my ideas into restaurant realities. Thanks, too, to Achilles and Michael, for being willing samplers and good critics of everything. Special thanks, too, to Brigitte Bernhardt Fatsio, for her thoroughness and fastidiousness when testing all the recipes.

Books are only as good as their editors, and I have a wonderful one, Harriet Bell, who has helped me over the years to bring abstract ideas to paper, bound and beautiful. Thanks, too, to the design team at William Morrow, for designing a gorgeous book.

ACKNOWLEDGMENTS

Over the last few years, I have partnered with my husband, Vassilis Stenos, on many projects. He shot the gorgeous, evocative photographs in this book, bringing all his training as a fine artist to the camera lens. Life and work would be drab without him. I want to say thanks, too, to Greece's premiere food stylist, Tina Webb, for lending her aesthetic know-how to each and every picture. The photographs were all shot under the Greek sun, in the bucolic, barbecue-ready haven known as Pendeli, just north of Athens.

My life would be nothing without family. My kids, Kyveli and Yiorgos, who licked their fingers at the grill, are my deepest joy and harshest critics. My sisters, Athena and Koko, who never want me to cook in their kitchens for fear of a monumental mess, are always willing partners at the table. I've savored more than a few backyard barbecues with them and their kids, George, Tom, Kristy and Katharine, and their husbands, Paul and Trif.

I can't begin to thank my friends, all of them, with whom I've shared many a table over the years. I count myself blessed for having so many close ones, but especially the Heights boys, Dan and Van.

Lastly, I want to thank my mom, Zoe, because her tenacity and perseverance have influenced me more than anything else in the world.

never anticipated how much fun it would be to write a grill book, mainly because grilling, especially in the Mediterranean, and especially in Greece, is a convivial pastime. Everything about it spawns friendly cooperation and warm, hedonistic pleasures.

This book was born in a small place we call home three months a year, in Raches, Ikaria, Greece. A few summers ago, we were housebound with a newborn and spent our nights in the garden of the 100-year-old house we rent. The garden is enclosed by an ancient stone wall with a cavernous, arched indentation in one spot. That was the al fresco barbecue of yore, the place where dinner would be cooked on a blackened old grill over bramble and vinewood. We used it, too, almost every night, grilling fresh island fish, marinated lamb, vegetables just picked from the garden, and more. We have peach, apricot, and plum trees on the property and the fruits they bear became fodder for the grill, too. Grilling turned into our evening entertainment, a wafting open invitation to friends and neighbors to come and join us, which they often did.

But my real baptism by fire into the ways of grilling happened under much more duress in the same 100-year-old house, when we decided, the next summer and the one

INTRODUCTION

that followed as well, to turn the place into a seasonal restaurant. I bought my first professional grill, a small gas-fired box filled with large ceramic shards that provided the steady heat needed to grill local goat cheese appetizers, pita bread galore, chops, pancetta, and vegetables. The pièce de résistance wasn't savory but sweet: grilled juicy peaches drizzled with honey syrup and cooled with a spoonful of fresh tart yogurt. We left tradition for the stewpot and used the grill to turn out fun, new food or classics with a twist. Grilled octopus with charred tomatoes, thick strips of ouzo-marinated pancetta that flared up and filled with kitchen with the intoxicating scent of anise, freshly made slabs of goat cheese grilled to a nanosecond before the melting point—all became house specialties. We closed the restaurant in the summer of 2003, but we kept the grill and still use it.

Greeks, of course, are no strangers to grilling. Grilling is arguably the oldest culinary art form in the Mediterranean, the vehicle of heroes' feasts and ancient rituals. There are tools still used today that have remained the same over the centuries: the *satz*, for example—a sheet of metal, basically a freeform griddle—was the tool of choice for ancient, often itinerant cooks throughout the Mediterranean and the Fertile Crescent. It's not much different from the hotplate used on indoor grills in today's ultramodern kitchens. Greek island cooks still use something called a *fou-fou*, which is basically a miniature clay or ceramic grill with a docked tray on top where the food sits and a space just beneath where a small fire burns that cooks the food on hand. Until a generation or two ago, it was the utensil most home cooks used to grill fish. My favorite Greek grilling accoutrement is a slightly more modern long-handled, cagelike contraption meant especially for whole fish, to keep it intact over the grill and to facilitate turning it without causing it to fall apart. Every taverna has one, and so do most home cooks. Another favorite tool is clearly seasonal, hawked on street corners and sold in upscale kitchen shops alike: the automated spit for roasting a whole lamb or goat at Easter. Before someone thought of attaching a battery-operated motor to the outdoor rotisserie, the job was usually shared by a handful of friends, mostly men, who'd begin early in the day by digging a shallow pit for the charcoal and placing the two ends of the rotisserie carefully over it. Threading the lamb or goat onto the rotisserie, whole from head to hoof, of course, was a job unto itself, taken over by the most experienced hands. Sausages and other spit-roasted specialties also followed. Greek Easter is as much a festival of spring as it is a religious and food feast. While the men tend the spit, the women cook copiously, serving up tray after tray of meze and wine. Conviviality and grilling always go hand in hand.

By far, though, my all-time favorite piece of grilling equipment is the makeshift barbecue that looks a little like a metal bassinet. It's the ultimate ad hoc creation, born of the sense of economy that's endemic in the Mediterranean. It's made by slicing in half lengthwise the large, cylindrical water heaters that adorn most Greek bathroom walls. Of course, people wait for the thing to break down beyond repair to turn it into a barbecue. But they do, indeed, and people put it on a stand, empty a sack full of charcoal into its belly, and fit a grill rack on top. It's not as sexy as a kettle grill, but it gets the job done and it proves the wisdom of an old Greek saying: you can learn to cook but you are born to grill. That is, you either have the talent or you don't, regardless of equipment.

That was my modus operandi when writing this book. Grilling isn't so much about meticulously following specific recipes as it is about communicating with the equipment at hand, knowing the heat, feeling it, using instinct more than acquired skills to turn out perfect meals. The recipes I offer in the following pages are a combination of traditional and contemporary Mediterranean grill specialties. In some, the grill is used as a means to a larger end—one or two ingredients in the final dish might be grilled, then used as parts of a whole, which might be a salad, a soup, or a pasta dish. In other recipes, especially meats and fish, the grill is usually the centerpiece. Everything in these pages is accessible and easy, the better to give the grillmaster time to tune in to the heat and adjust his or her instincts to the sputtering, searing object of dinner.

GRILLING IN THE MEDITERRANEAN

From the meshwi and ground meat kofte of the Middle East to the great kebabs of Turkey to the bistecca alla Florentina of Italy to France's grillades and famed chateaubriand, grilled delicacies are part of every culture of the Mediterranean. The flavors of grilled foods throughout the Mediterranean are often intense and highly aromatic; marinades and spice rubs include everything from yogurt to citrus fruits to the myriad herbs growing under the Mediterranean sun. The meats—lamb, veal, chicken, pork, game birds, etc., are truly succulent. The grill also serves the fisherman's bounty from this most famous of seas. All over the Mediterranean, fish is charred to smoky perfection either whole on the bone or skewered, or wrapped and char-grilled, as in the grape-leaf–rolled whole sardines in Greece, southern France, and parts of Italy.

There is a similarity in technique but a vast variety of individual flavors in the grilled foods of the Mediterranean. A Syrian barbecue feast, for example, might include spit-roasted lamb, fragrant with ginger, sage, marjoram, and olive oil, or skewered bite-size pieces of lamb marinated with wine and mint. In Turkey, the same grilled lamb might be marinated in yogurt and herbs. In Greece, grilled lamb is almost always synonymous with the Pascal feast, but farther west, in Provence, a boned and butterflied leg of lamb best exemplifies the local traditions.

Grilling crosses all cultural and religious boundaries in the Middle East, and it is both the domain of specialized restaurants and something people do at home, often for festive occasions. In Israel, every holiday involves Israeli families setting up *mangals*, which are portable little square grills on which they cook all sorts of small-cut meats. There is also a great affinity for restaurants that specialize in meat on skewers. A delicacy at one of them in Tel Aviv is goose liver on skewers. There's a whole neighborhood of grill restaurants in Tel Aviv, called Schchunat Hatikva, or the "Neighborhood of Hope." Among Arabs, the *meshwa*, or grill, is also the centerpiece of festive occasions. Such feasts often take place on Fridays, the Muslim holy day, as well as on weekends, when people take to the countryside for picnic feasts. In Greece, festive grilling culminates in the spit-roasted Easter lamb.

The grilling traditions date back to the most ancient times, to the feasts of mythological heroes, to the sacrificial lamb that was part of every culture from Mesopotamia to Ancient Rome. But it is not a tradition limited to the eastern Mediterranean. Indeed, some of the most delicious dishes are Italian, French, and Spanish. One of my favorite meals in the world is the elaborate rolled *involtini*, made with meat or fish, a specialty of southern Italy. Unlike skewered dishes in the eastern Mediterranean, these are dipped in batter before being grilled. In Provence, the *grillades*—basically steaks slathered in olive oil, then seared on a barbecue—are among the most familiar dishes. The French also gave us one of the world's most famous grilled meat preparations, chateaubriand.

While the sound and smells of meat sizzling on a grill are always enticing, meat, fish, and poultry are not the only barbecued specialties in the Mediterranean. In Egypt, one of the most delicious treats of all is Jerusalem artichokes marinated and roasted to perfection over hot embers. The garlic-and-herb–infused eggplants, zucchini, peppers, and more culled from Italian and Provençal traditions have become part of our daily food culture in the United States. Many baked vegetable dishes also begin on the grill, such as savory grilled eggplant moussaka, or grilled eggplant, zucchini, and/or pepper timbales baked with cheese.

In Greece, there is a special holiday devoted to grilled foods—Tsiknopempti, which roughly translates to "Smoky Thursday." It takes place on the third Thursday of Carnival, ten days before the start of Lent. It is one of the busiest restaurant nights of the year. The tavernas are full. Grillmen—they are almost always men—prep mountains of lamb chops, sausages, ribs, kebabs, ground meat specialties, and more. There is a particular tang in the air, a scent that wafts from restaurant and home kitchens alike. It's the holy trinity of Greek marinades—garlic, oregano, and lemon—tempering the cool March air.

Not until summer, when fish becomes king of the grill, does grilling take center stage again. And what would the Mediterranean table be without the most classic of all grilled foods, those myriad cubes of meats, fish, seafood, and vegetables threaded onto skewers and grilled? Souvlaki, kabob, spedini, pincitos, and more—these are among the timeless classics of the Mediterranean grill; they are foods that have acted as virtual ambassadors, ushering Mediterranean cooking into every corner of the world.

A WORD ON EQUIPMENT

Most of the recipes in this book are flexible enough in their approach so that the ingredients can be grilled on anything from a portable hibachi to a wall-size restaurant grill. Most dishes were tested on a simple gas grill as well as on a simple charcoal grill. Food grilled over charcoal definitely tastes better than food grilled over gas. Popular Mediterranean dishes like grilled fish and grilled eggplant wouldn't have the universal appeal they enjoy if it weren't for the intense flavor of the smoke that infuses them.

Grilling to perfection follows a pretty simple principle: the higher the heat, the faster something is apt to sear—or burn. It usually takes about 15 minutes for charcoal to reach the red-hot ember stage once it's lit, and about a half hour to 45 minutes for the heat to die down enough so that the coals are safe to cook over without burning the food. High heat is good for searing and charring thick cuts of meat, which call for a crisp surface and a rare tender interior, and some vegetables, but mostly I prefer to grill over moderate heat. Some foods, such as grilled pizza, need either low heat or a closed lid with open air holes.

I use the time-tested method for knowing when the coals are ready: I hold my hand, palm side down, about 6 inches from the grill rack. If you can hold it there for about 5 seconds, the heat is high; for 10 seconds, the heat is medium; and for 15 seconds, the heat is low. I also adjust the heat on the grill by shifting the coals: the more there are on one spot, obviously the hotter the grill, and vice versa. Generally, when using a charcoal grill, light the charcoal fire and let it wane until the coals are covered with white ash. The grill rack, standard on most grills, should be about 4 to 6 inches from the heat source.

Every grill and barbecue, just like every oven, has its idiosyncracies. Observation and instinct are the ultimate guides when grilling.

MEDITERRANEAN FLAVORS

Probably the single greatest aspect of grilling in the Mediterranean is the gamut of flavors that season dishes from one end of the basin to the other. Thinly sliced raw onion, olive oil, and chili peppers characterize many of the grilled dishes of Turkey, while in neighboring Greece the quartet of olive oil, lemon juice, garlic, and herbs infuses grilled meats, fish, and vegetables. The sweet, aromatic spices of North Africa, especially Morocco, and the earthy, robust, pepper-and-garlic spiced dishes of Spain complete the spectrum.

Marinades throughout the Mediterranean are both wet and dry, comprising wines, liqueurs, citrus juices, and herbs, but also the heady flavors of strong spices such as cinnamon, cumin, and turmeric. Sweet and sour combinations, made with honey, sweet wine, or grape syrup and a whole range of vinegars and citrus juices, add another note to the rich tapestry of Mediterranean flavors. Liquid seasonings work both as marinades and as sauces and dipping condiments; dry flavor combinations are usually pulverized in the traditional way, inside a mortar with a pestle.

Mediterranean grilled foods are by and large easy to make, accessible, and healthy. As with any single cooking method, however, organization is the key—all the more so when the main piece of equipment usually stands outside the kitchen. Once the grill is fired up and the heat is at the level you want it, have everything you need nearby, within arm's reach. Some of the recipes in this book call for using the grill in one step of an overall recipe, so shuttling back and forth between the kitchen and the deck or backyard or balcony means you have to be doubly well organized. Grilling requires patience and the ability to keep constant watch over what's being cooked. After a while, as with driving and riding a bicycle, the timing becomes second nature.

SALADS

fresh off the grill

A grilled salad might seem like a contradiction in terms, especially in the Mediterranean, where salads are usually equated with the freshest, crispest textures and a minimum of intervention.

Most of the salads in this chapter can easily stand on their own as main courses, although most were developed while the grill was already on for something else. Although they are by and large filling, the salads are in fact meant to be prepared while you are cooking something else on the grill. I am too much of a home economist to suggest lighting the grill just for a salad.

Grilled fruit is something I have come to love, mainly because grilling brings out a whole new battery of flavor elements in fruit. I use grilled fruit in several salads, especially as a contrast with other ingredients, such as grilled pears with peppery arugula and grilled oranges, which become slightly bitter, together with grilled onions, which turn slightly sweet because of the caramelization, coupled with juicy, fleshy grilled red peppers.

The best salads are a whole world of varied tastes and textures tossed together in a bowl, and grilling provides a way to differentiate certain ingredients. Grains such as bulgur wheat go exceptionally well with a range of grilled vegetables, and beans, one of the mainstays of the Mediterranean salad bowl, where so much is served at room temperature, are a cook's carte blanche to add almost anything that strikes his or her fancy.

Everything that's important in the Mediterranean is in evidence in the salad bowl, with the dressings running throughout like a stream of flavor constants. Olive oil, of course, appears in every recipe; vinaigrettes can be as simple as the trio of the region's green gold, balsamic, and salt and pepper or as multifaceted as a citrus-laced sauce with chopped fresh herbs, or a honey-sweetened, chili-spiked elixir, or even one enriched with crumbled feta cheese.

There really is only one rule when making Mediterranean salads, grilled or otherwise: use the freshest possible ingredients and the best extra virgin olive oil.

1

ARUGULA SALAD WITH GRILLED PEARS, PISTACHIOS, AND RICOTTA SALATA

GRILLED FRUIT is a newcomer to the traditional Mediterranean table. This dish was inspired by a friend and chef, Nena Ismirnoglou, and then adapted by me for the menu at Pylos, a Greek restaurant in Manhattan's East Village.

MAKES 4 SERVINGS

1 cup shelled pistachios

4 large pears, peeled, cored, and halved

2 tablespoons extra virgin olive oil

4 (1/3-inch-thick) round slices ricotta salata or Greek manouri cheese

8 cups trimmed, torn arugula leaves

For the dressing

1/4 cup extra virgin olive oil

4 tablespoons honey

4 tablespoons balsamic vinegar

2 tablespoons fresh orange juice

1 teaspoon chopped fresh thyme

1/2 teaspoon crushed pink peppercorns

Salt and freshly ground black pepper to taste

Heat the grill to medium.

Place the pistachios in a shallow, heavy pan and place on the grill rack. Pull down the lid (make sure the ventilation holes are open), and smoke for about 3 minutes. Open the lid once, shake the pan back and forth to keep the nuts from burning, and continue smoking another minute or two, until lightly browned. Remove and set aside.

In a medium bowl, toss the pears with the olive oil. Place on the hottest part of the grill rack, turning, until there are light grill marks on each of the pear wedges, about 3 minutes. Remove.

Place the cheese rounds on the grill rack over a medium-hot spot on the grill and cook just until the cheese is branded lightly with grill lines. Flip carefully and repeat on the other side. Remove.

Divide the arugula evenly among four plates. Cut each cheese round into quarters. Top the arugula with alternating wedges of grilled ricotta salata and grilled pears. Add the smoked pistachios.

Make the dressing: Whisk together all the dressing ingredients until smooth and pour in equal amounts over each salad. Serve.

GRILLED GREEN BEAN SALAD
WITH CHARRED TOMATOES AND FETA VINAIGRETTE

BASED ON A TRIED-AND-TRUE traditional Greek stew, the same ingredients take on a decidedly different character when they are grilled. The stew is often served with a wedge of feta on the side. Here, the cheese becomes part of the dressing.

MAKES 4 TO 6 SERVINGS

1 pound large, fresh green beans, trimmed

1 cup extra virgin olive oil

Sea salt to taste

1 medium head garlic

2 large red onions, each cut into 4 to 6 thick slices

4 medium, firm, ripe tomatoes, quartered

2/3 cup fresh basil leaves, cut into thin ribbons

4 tablespoons red wine vinegar

Freshly ground black pepper to taste

1/3 cup crumbled Greek feta

Heat the grill to medium.

Bring a large pot of salted water to a rolling boil and blanch the green beans for about 3 minutes, until al dente. Remove and submerge in an ice-water bath. Drain, pat dry, and toss with 3 tablespoons of the olive oil and a little salt.

Wrap the garlic in aluminum foil and place on the grill. Brush the onion slices with about 2 tablespoons olive oil and place them on the grill together with the garlic. Do the same with the tomatoes: brush them with 2 to 3 tablespoons of olive oil and place them on the grill next to the onions. Close the lid on the grill (make sure the ventilation holes are open) and smoke the garlic, onions, and tomatoes for about 20 minutes, or until the tomatoes and onions are lightly caramelized. The tomatoes will take longer than the onions and the garlic will take the longest.

Place the beans on the grill, leaving the lid and grill just until the beans acquire grill marks, about 3 minutes. Turn once, being careful not to push the beans through the grill rack. Remove and place in a serving bowl. Coarsely chop the grilled onion slices and the tomatoes and add to the beans. Squeeze half the smoked garlic cloves into the salad and add the basil leaves.

In a small separate bowl, add the remaining olive oil, the vinegar, sea salt, pepper, and crumbled feta and squeeze in the remaining smoked garlic cloves. Whisk until smooth. Pour the dressing over the salad, toss gently, and serve.

SPANISH WARM GRILLED VEGETABLE SALAD

HERE IS A FILLING salad that's a great accompaniment to grilled meats and fish and works well tossed into the pasta bowl, too.

MAKES 6 SERVINGS

Vegetable oil for brushing grill rack

½ cup extra virgin olive oil, plus extra for brushing onion

Salt and freshly ground black pepper to taste

2 large eggplants, about 1 pound each, cut into ½-inch rounds

2 medium-large zucchini, cut into ½-inch rounds

1 small head garlic

3 large red bell peppers

1 large white onion, unpeeled

For the vinaigrette

⅓ cup extra virgin olive oil

3 tablespoons sherry vinegar

2 tablespoons minced flat-leaf parsley leaves

Heat the grill to medium-high and oil the grill rack.

Combine the olive oil with salt and pepper in a bowl large enough to hold the eggplants and zucchini. Add the vegetables and toss. Let the vegetables stand for 20 minutes.

Grill the garlic, peppers, and onion first, since they will take the longest. Wrap the garlic in aluminum foil, enclosing it completely. Place in a corner of the grill, over indirect heat, and grill for about 25 minutes, until the cloves are very tender. Place the peppers on the grill in a medium-hot spot, and grill for 15 to 20 minutes, turning, until charred on all sides and very soft. Cut the onion in half, brush with a little olive oil, and place cut side down on the coolest part of the grill. Grill for 15 to 20 minutes, turning, until lightly charred and soft.

Place the eggplant and zucchini slices on the grill and grill, turning once, until browned and grill-marked, 8 to 10 minutes.

Peel and seed the grilled peppers. Cut into 1-inch chunks. Cut the eggplant, zucchini, and onion into 1-inch pieces. Place all the vegetables in a bowl. Squeeze the softened pulp from the garlic cloves. Add to the vegetables.

Make the vinaigrette: Whisk together the olive oil, vinegar, and parsley, then toss with the vegetables. Serve.

GRILLED COLORED PEPPER SALAD WITH HERB-FLAVORED OLIVE OIL

WE GROW ALL sorts of peppers on our little patch of land in Ikaria each summer. I sometimes make this salad without the prosciutto and with mild local goat's milk cheese instead of mozzarella. You can substitute another Italian cured ham, such as bresaola, or Iberian cured ham for the prosciutto.

MAKES 4 TO 6 SERVINGS

1/2 cup extra virgin olive oil, plus 2 tablespoons for brushing peppers

2 fresh thyme sprigs

1 fresh rosemary sprig

1/3 cup fresh basil leaves

10 whole black peppercorns

3 yellow bell peppers

3 red bell peppers

16 wrinkled black Moroccan olives

Sea salt to taste

6 slices prosciutto, trimmed

12 ounces fresh mozzarella in water, cut into 1/4-inch rounds

1 to 2 tablespoons balsamic vinegar

Warm the 1/2 cup olive oil over low heat in a skillet. Pour into a heatproof glass container and add the herbs and peppercorns. Seal and let stand at least 2 hours, but preferably overnight. (The oil may be made in larger batches and kept on hand indefinitely if stored in a cool, dark place.)

Heat the grill to medium. Rub the peppers with the 2 tablespoons olive oil and grill over medium heat, turning, until their skins char and crack, about 25 minutes. Place the olives in a small, shallow pan on a hot part of the grill and grill for 10 to 12 minutes, until they dehydrate a little. Their flavor will intensify and turn slightly smoky.

Remove the olives and set aside. When the peppers are charred and cracked all over, remove from the grill to a bowl, cover with plastic wrap, and let stand for about 15 minutes to cool. Peel the peppers, remove their seeds, and cut into 1½ to 2-inch strips. Drain the pepper juices and set aside.

Have a large serving platter ready. Place the red peppers on the bottom of the plate, fanning them out in a circle. Sprinkle lightly with sea salt. Place the prosciutto over them. Next, layer the yellow peppers in the same way, sprinkling lightly with sea salt. Follow with the cheese, layered over the yellow peppers in an overlapping, fanlike circle. Finally, top with the olives. Pour the flavored olive oil, pepper juice, and a little balsamic over the salad and serve.

CHUNKY GRILLED ROOT VEGETABLE SALAD

THE EARTHINESS of all root vegetables becomes enhanced when the vegetables are grilled.

MAKES 6 TO 8 SERVINGS

1 small celery root

2 large carrots, peeled and cut in half lengthwise

1 large fennel bulb

2 medium onions

1 large leek, trimmed and cut into 2-inch cylinders

3 medium beets

7 tablespoons extra virgin olive oil

Sea salt and freshly ground black pepper to taste

3 tablespoons balsamic vinegar or strained fresh lemon juice

2 tablespoon chopped fresh basil

Heat the grill to medium.

Using a chef's knife, cut away the rough outer layer of the celery root. Quarter the celery root into wedges, then slice each wedge into $3/4$-inch pieces. Cut the carrots into four cylindrical pieces, lengthwise. Bring a large pot of salted water to a rolling boil and blanch the carrots and celery root together for about 12 minutes. Remove with a slotted spoon. Do not discard the water.

While the carrots and celery root are blanching, trim the fennel bulb, removing the stalks and feathery leaves. In the same water as the celery root and carrots, blanch the fennel bulb, onions, and leek for about 8 minutes, until translucent and softened. Remove with a slotted spoon, cool, and then cut the fennel into wedges or thick slices and the onion in half.

Next, trim and peel the beets. Cut into wedges. Bring the water back to a boil and blanch the beets for 7 to 8 minutes. Remove and drain. Toss the fennel, onions, and leek in a bowl with 2 tablespoons of olive oil and some sea salt.

Remove the fennel, onions, and leeks with a slotted spoon and place on the grill over direct heat. These vegetables will need about 15 minutes of grilling time. Keep them over direct heat for about 5 minutes, then move them to the sides of the grill rack to make room for the next batch of vegetables.

While the fennel, onions, and leek are grilling, toss the carrots, celery root, and beets in 2 tablespoons of olive oil and some sea salt. Place on the grill over direct heat, and grill for about 10 minutes, turning once.

When the vegetables are grilled through, remove to a bowl. Cut the onion halves into quarters. Toss all the grilled vegetables with the remaining 3 tablespoons olive oil, salt, pepper, and balsamic vinegar or lemon juice. Sprinkle with the basil and serve.

GRILLED SHRIMP, PEPPER, AND PEACH SALAD

PEACHES AND PEPPERS are combined in this delicious salad from Turkey. The peaches and peppers share a similar smooth, slippery texture but their distinctly different flavors provide a nice contrast. Try this dish with scallops instead of shrimp, or even with grilled lobster.

MAKES 4 SERVINGS

Vegetable oil for brushing grill rack

3 firm, ripe freestone peaches, peeled and pitted

2 scant tablespoons sugar

1 fresh hot red chili pepper, seeded and cut into very thin slices

2 tablespoons fresh mint leaves, cut into thin ribbons

2 teaspoons ground cumin

2 to 3 tablespoons strained fresh lemon juice

3 green bell peppers

1½ pounds large shrimp, peeled, deveined, and heads removed but with tails attached

6 tablespoons extra virgin olive oil

Salt and white pepper to taste

Heat the grill to medium and lightly oil the grill rack.

Cut each peach into 8 slices. Place in a medium serving bowl and toss with the sugar, chili pepper, mint, 1 teaspoon cumin, and 1 tablespoon lemon juice. Set aside.

Place the bell peppers on the grill over direct heat and grill until browned and soft, turning to char lightly on all sides. Remove, cool slightly, peel, and seed. Cut the peppers lengthwise into 1-inch strips.

While the peppers are grilling, toss the shrimp with 2 tablespoons olive oil. Place over a hot part of the grill and cook, turning once, until they change color and are marked with grill marks on both sides. Remove.

Toss the peppers and shrimp together with the peaches in the serving bowl. Season with salt, pepper, the remaining teaspoon cumin, and the remaining 4 tablespoons olive oil. Add the remaining 1 to 2 tablespoons lemon juice if desired. Serve.

TABBOULEH WITH ARUGULA, GRILLED ONIONS, ORANGE, AND RED PEPPER

BULGUR WHEAT is one of my favorite grains. Here's an alternative to traditional tabbouleh, with arugula in lieu of chopped parsley and grilled peppers instead of tomatoes. This goes nicely with grilled seafood.

MAKES 6 TO 8 SERVINGS

2 cups coarse bulgur wheat

1 large red onion, quartered

1 small orange, peeled and cut into sections

2 large red bell peppers

1/3 cup extra virgin olive oil

1/2 cup whole pitted Kalamata olives

2 cups fresh arugula, rinsed and finely chopped

For the dressing

1/2 cup extra virgin olive oil

1/4 cup strained fresh orange juice

2 to 3 tablespoons strained fresh lemon juice

1 to 2 tablespoons Tabasco sauce, or to taste (optional)

Salt and freshly ground black pepper to taste

Soak the bulgur in a medium bowl in 3 cups water for 1 hour, or until most of the water is absorbed. (You can do this in the morning and find the bulgur ready to use when you return from work.) Line a colander with a double layer of paper towels and drain the bulgur, patting down with additional paper towels to absorb any excess water. Set aside.

Heat the grill to medium. Toss the onion, orange sections, and red bell peppers with the olive oil. Grill over medium heat until each ingredient is lightly charred and the peppers are softened and charred. The peppers will take about 25 minutes. The onion wedges should take 12 to 15 minutes. The orange slices will take just a few minutes.

Remove the onion, orange sections, and peppers as they grill. Let the peppers stand in a shallow bowl, covered with plastic wrap, until cool enough to handle. Peel, seed, and coarsely chop. Save the pepper juice. Dice the onion and orange sections.

Place the olives on a small metal baking dish and cover with aluminum foil. Place on the grill, pull the grill cover down (make sure the air vents are open), and smoke the olives for 6 to 8 minutes over the coolest part of the grill. If using a gas grill set at medium, smoke them for about 5 minutes. Coarsely chop the olives.

In a serving bowl combine the olives, grilled vegetables, oranges, and arugula.

Make the dressing: In a small bowl, combine the olive oil, reserved pepper juices, orange and lemon juices, Tabasco, salt, and pepper. Whisk until smooth and add to the vegetable mixture. Toss to combine. Add the bulgur and fluff with a fork. Allow the salad to stand for 10 to 20 minutes in the refrigerator. Remove and serve.

CHICKPEA SALAD WITH GRILLED EGGPLANT AND TAHINI DRESSING

THIS DISH TAKES its cue from an old Turkish and Greek recipe for chickpeas baked or stewed with eggplant. It's a dish found in many regions of the eastern Mediterranean, among many disparate populations, Arab, Jewish, and Christian alike. I have changed it to make it a salad with grilled eggplant, and have borrowed from the Arab culinary traditions for the dressing, which uses tahini, an ingredient often coupled with eggplant and chickpeas, albeit in dips and spreads.

MAKES 4 TO 6 SERVINGS

2 medium eggplants

Salt

$1/2$ cup extra virgin olive oil

3 cups canned chickpeas, rinsed and drained

1 cup finely chopped fresh flat-leaf parsley or cilantro

For the dressing

2 large garlic cloves, minced

$1/2$ teaspoon salt, or more to taste

3 tablespoons tahini

3 to 5 tablespoons lemon juice

$1/3$ cup extra virgin olive oil

Paprika or cayenne pepper for garnish

Prepare the eggplants. Cut them into $1/2$-inch-wide lengthwise slices and layer in a colander with a little salt. Place a weight over the eggplant to press out any bitter juices. Let them stand in the salt for 25 to 30 minutes. Remove. It is not necessary to rinse the eggplant after salting.

Heat the grill to medium. Brush the eggplant slices on one side with olive oil and place that side face down on the grill. Grill until softened and marked with grill lines on the bottom, 8 to 10 minutes. Turn, brush with more olive oil, and grill on the flip side until lined and softened. Remove from the grill and let cool for a few minutes. Cut the eggplant into 1-inch squares.

Place the chickpeas, eggplant, and parsley in a serving bowl and toss gently.

Make the dressing: Combine the garlic and salt in the bowl of a food processor and pulse on and off for a few seconds until the garlic is a paste. Add the tahini, 3 tablespoons lemon juice, olive oil, and $1/3$ cup water. Process until smooth. Add more lemon juice, water, and salt as needed or desired. The consistency should be that of a thick, creamy salad dressing. Pour over the salad, mix gently, and serve, sprinkled with a light dusting of paprika or cayenne.

TABBOULEH WITH GRILLED ASPARAGUS, MINT, AND PINE NUTS

THIS SALAD IS A LOVELY accompaniment to almost all the grilled meats and fish in these pages and works well as a vegetarian component to an all-vegetable grilled meal.

MAKES 4 TO 6 SERVINGS

1½ cups coarse bulgur wheat

10 to 12 thin asparagus stalks

4 scallions or springs onions, trimmed but left whole

½ cup extra virgin olive oil, or more as needed

Salt to taste

½ cup pine nuts or blanched almonds

1 garlic clove, minced

⅔ cup finely chopped fresh mint leaves

⅔ cup finely chopped fresh parsley

3 tablespoons strained fresh lemon juice, or more as needed

Freshly ground black pepper to taste

Place the bulgur in a bowl and pour in 2 cups water. Cover and let soak for about 1 hour, or until the water is absorbed. Empty into a bowl lined with a double layer of paper towels. Fold the paper towels over the bulgur and squeeze out the excess moisture. (You can also prepare the bulgur according to package directions, by boiling an equal quantity of water, adding the bulgur, closing the lid, and letting it stand for 5 minutes.)

Heat the grill to medium. As the grill is heating, bring a medium pot of salted water to a rolling boil and blanch the asparagus for 2 minutes. Remove with a slotted spoon and place in an ice-water bath immediately. Drain and pat dry.

Brush the asparagus and scallions with a little olive oil and salt and place on the grill over medium heat. Grill until soft but al dente and until the asparagus and scallions have acquired grill marks, 10 to 12 minutes. Sprinkle with salt and remove. Cut both into ½-inch pieces.

Season the bulgur lightly with salt and toss. Add the asparagus and scallions. Place the pine nuts in a dry skillet, either on the grill or on the stovetop, and toast lightly. Add to the bulgur. Add the garlic, mint, parsley, remaining olive oil, the lemon juice, and pepper. Toss, adjust seasoning with additional salt, pepper, and olive oil and lemon juice if needed. Let stand at room temperature for 20 minutes before serving.

GRILLED CORN AND POTATO SALAD WITH PURSLANE AND CHERRY TOMATOES

THIS COLORFUL summer salad is perfect as a vegetarian main course. Purslane grows wild in many a backyard throughout North America. You just have to recognize its succulent leaves. You can also find it via specialty produce vendors, online, and in some gourmet shops.

MAKES 4 TO 6 SERVINGS

2 large ears fresh corn

4 large boiling potatoes, scrubbed and trimmed

$^2/_3$ cup extra virgin olive oil

Salt

1 large red onion, coarsely chopped

$^1/_2$ pound vine-ripened cherry tomatoes, stems removed, halved

$^1/_2$ cup fresh Italian basil leaves, cut into thin ribbons

$^1/_4$ cup flat-leaf parsley leaves, finely chopped

2 cups purslane, trimmed and broken into 2-inch pieces

2 hard-boiled eggs

2 to 3 tablespoons sherry vinegar

Freshly ground black pepper to taste

Remove the husks from the corn. Bring a large pot of salted water to a rolling boil and drop in the corn. Blanch until tender but al dente, 8 to 10 minutes. Remove with a slotted spoon and set aside. In the same water, boil the potatoes for about 20 minutes, until firm and about three-quarters of the way cooked. They should be pierceable but firm enough to cut into thick slices without falling apart. Remove from the water with a slotted spoon and submerge into an ice-water bath. When the potatoes are cool enough to handle, remove, peel, and cut each potato into four thick oval lengthwise slices. While the potatoes are blanching, heat the grill to medium-hot.

Gather the potatoes with the corn and olive oil and set them near the grill.

Brush the corn and potato slices with olive oil, season lightly with salt, and grill until the potatoes are tender but firm and lined with grill marks and the corn is lightly charred, about 5 minutes. Remove.

Let the corn cool slightly, then using a sharp paring knife, cut off the kernels into a serving bowl. Cut the potato slices into $^1/_2$-inch cubes. Don't worry if the potatoes fall apart slightly—add every last bit of them to the serving bowl. Add the onion, tomatoes, basil, parsley, and purslane. Peel and cut the hard-boiled eggs into quarters and add to the top of the salad.

Whisk together the remaining olive oil and the vinegar and season with salt and pepper. Pour over the salad. Toss gently and serve.

GRILLED CHICKEN SALAD WITH RAISINS, ORANGE, FENNEL, AND LETTUCE

ORANGE AND FENNEL are a classic, pan-Mediterranean duo. Here is a main-course salad that is perfect for summer lunch or brunch.

MAKES 4 TO 6 SERVINGS

½ cup extra virgin olive oil

½ cup strained fresh orange juice

2 tablespoons strained fresh lemon juice

2 teaspoons Dijon mustard

2 tablespoons finely chopped fresh mint

Salt and freshly ground black pepper to taste

1 pound boneless, skinless chicken breasts

1 medium fennel bulb, trimmed and quartered

1 medium orange, peeled and quartered

2 heads Boston Bibb lettuce, trimmed, torn, washed, and spun-dry

¼ cup fresh mint leaves, cut into thin ribbons

3 tablespoons golden raisins, plumped in ⅓ cup warm water

6 tablespoons extra virgin olive oil

2 tablespoons balsamic vinegar

In a medium bowl, whisk together the olive oil, orange and lemon juices, mustard, mint, salt, and pepper. Toss the chicken, fennel, and orange quarters in the mixture, cover with plastic wrap, and leave to marinate 1 hour in the refrigerator. Remove and leave at room temperature for about 20 minutes.

In the meantime, heat the grill to medium-hot.

Grill the chicken on the hottest part of the grill to sear it. Shift the coals or adjust the heat to medium, and grill the fennel and orange quarters on a medium-hot part of the grill. Turn the fennel and orange sections once to grill on both sides and remove when tender. The chicken needs about 8 minutes on each side. The fennel will take 7 to 8 minutes. The orange will take the least amount of time, 3 to 4 minutes. Brush all three with the marinade as you grill them. Remove and set aside. (If you are using a gas grill with more even heat distribution, set the grill to medium and keep a close tab on the timing.)

Place the lettuce and mint on a large serving platter. Strain the raisins and discard their liquid. Set the raisins aside. In a small bowl, whisk together the olive oil, balsamic vinegar, and salt and pepper until smooth.

Cut the chicken breasts into 1-inch-wide strips. Coarsely chop the fennel and slice the orange sections. Place the fennel over the lettuce, then the grilled chicken strips; sprinkle with the orange slices and raisins. Pour the dressing over the salad and serve.

BEAN SALAD WITH GRILLED SHRIMP AND SAUSAGES

WHEN MY FRIEND Brigitte, a German who's been living in Greece for twenty-odd years, tested this recipe for me, she used a German raw pork sausage, blanched it and then grilled it, to rave reviews. The combination of shrimp, beans, sausage, and vegetables makes this salad perfect as a main course or, in smaller portions, as a starter.

MAKES 4 TO 6 SERVINGS

½ pound dried navy beans, soaked overnight in water to cover, or 2 (16-ounce) cans good-quality beans

Salt to taste

⅓ cup extra virgin olive oil, or more to taste

Vegetable oil for brushing grill rack

1 pound fresh Italian sausage

2 red bell peppers

2 large red onions, cut lengthwise in half and then into 4 wedges per half

1½ pounds medium shrimp, peeled, deveined, and tails removed

Freshly ground black pepper to taste

3 to 4 tablespoons strained fresh lemon juice

2 garlic cloves, very finely chopped

½ cup chopped fresh flat-leaf parsley

If using dried beans, drain and place in a pot. Add water and bring to a boil; simmer for about 1 hour, or until cooked through but al dente. Ten minutes before removing from the heat, add the salt. Remove and drain in a colander under cold water. If using canned beans, rinse and drain in a colander. Place in a serving bowl and toss with half the olive oil.

Heat the grill to medium-hot and oil the grill rack.

Grill the sausage over a hot part of the grill for about 10 minutes, or until browned and slightly charred. On the same grill rack, grill the whole peppers and onion wedges, turning until lightly charred all over. Remove the peppers, cool for 5 minutes, peel, seed, and coarsely chop. Remove the onions and coarsely chop. Remove the sausage and cut into ¼-inch rounds. Place the chopped peppers, onions, and sausage in the bowl with the beans. Toss to combine.

Toss the shrimp with salt and pepper and grill over indirect heat for 3 to 4 minutes on each side. Add to the beans and mix. Add in the remaining olive oil, the lemon juice, garlic, additional salt and pepper to taste, and the parsley. Toss and serve.

WHITE BEAN SALAD WITH GRILLED SHRIMP, ZUCCHINI, AND ONIONS

BEANS GO well with all sorts of grilled vegetables. My favorites are zucchini and eggplant.

MAKES 4 SERVINGS

1/3 pound dried navy or cannellini beans, soaked overnight in water to cover, or 1 (15 1/2-ounce) can

1 bay leaf, cracked

4 medium zucchini

Salt and freshly ground black pepper to taste

1/2 cup chopped fresh flat-leaf parsley

Juice of 2 large lemons, or more to taste

6 tablespoons extra virgin olive oil, or more to taste

1 pound medium shrimp, peeled and deveined

1/2 teaspoon cayenne pepper, or more to taste

Vegetable oil for brushing grill rack

8 large scallions, trimmed

2 tablespoons snipped fresh dill

2 tablespoons small capers, rinsed and drained

Heat the grill to medium-hot.

Do all the kitchen prep before returning to the grill. Drain the soaked beans and place them in a large pot of cold water and bring to a boil. Add the bay leaf. Reduce the heat and simmer the beans, uncovered, for about 1 hour, or until tender without disintegrating. Remove from the heat, drain, and rinse in a colander under cold water. Remove the bay leaf. Set the beans aside. If using canned beans, empty into a colander and rinse with cold water.

Cut the zucchini lengthwise into 1/4-inch-thick slices and season with salt and pepper.

Combine the beans, parsley, half the lemon juice, and 3 tablespoons olive oil in a serving bowl. Set aside. Toss the shrimp with the remaining 3 tablespoons olive oil, remaining lemon juice, salt, pepper, and cayenne.

Oil the grill rack. Place the zucchini and scallions on the grill, and grill until lightly charred and marked, about 2 minutes per side. Remove. Cut the grilled scallions into thirds or quarters. Grill the shrimp, turning, for a total of 3 to 5 minutes, or until bright pink and cooked through.

Toss the shrimp, scallions, and zucchini with the beans. Add the dill and capers. Season with salt and pepper. Adjust the seasoning with additional olive oil, lemon juice, or cayenne as desired.

GRILLED
from the garden

Most cooked vegetable dishes in the Mediterranean are stewed, sautéed, turned into soups, or joined with meat, poultry, or seafood in a wide range of casseroles. Unlike traditional indoor Mediterranean cooking, which boasts an endless range of main-course vegetable dishes, Mediterranean-style grilled vegetables are usually served as appetizers, side dishes, or accompaniments to the main meal. With a few exceptions, grilled vegetables are relative newcomers to the Mediterranean table.

Among the vegetables that have long been favored for the grill are artichokes and eggplants. One of the great springtime treats in Greece and Spain, for example, is grilled artichokes with extra virgin olive oil and local seasonings. The slightly sour, grassy flavor of fresh artichokes mellows considerably when the vegetable is tamed by smoke.

It's no surprise that so many timeless Mediterranean dishes call for char-grilled eggplant. The vegetable thrives on smoke, and the duet of velvety flesh and char-grilled flavor is something I never get tired of. Eggplant is often grilled with an ulterior end in mind; that is, to be used as a component in something else, such as the classic Greek *melitzanosalata* and the Arabic *babaganoush*. In the pages that follow, I use it in much the same way, as a component, but in rolled or layered dishes, not purées.

Mushrooms are neither vegetables nor something usually found under a tree in a typical Mediterranean garden. They're foraged for in the wild, and to this day they make for one of the best treats the Mediterranean has to offer. I serve them in this chapter because they belong here more than anywhere else and because they fit the bill as an excellent first course, side dish, or accompaniment.

Since the weather stays warmer longer in the Mediterranean than it does in most parts of the United States, leeks, pumpkins, and sweet potatoes flood the market when most people are still wearing tee-shirts. These particular vegetables are often sautéed, stewed, or baked even in the Mediterranean, but they are also exceptional when grilled.

SMOKED GREEK GARDEN PACKETS

THIS DISH is inspired by a classic Greek summer dish called briam, which is a pan of thinly sliced seasonal vegetables—mainly potatoes, zucchini, peppers, and tomatoes—baked with plenty of olive oil. Briam often goes hand-in-hand with a side of feta cheese. Here, I have reworked the dish for the grill and called forth another typical Greek and pan-Mediterranean technique for wrapping foods in small individual packets before baking. The result looks lovely and the packets may be prepared several hours ahead and tossed on the grill on a moment's notice.

MAKES 6 SERVINGS

3/4 cup extra virgin olive oil

1 teaspoon Dijon mustard

Salt and freshly ground black pepper to taste

1 scant teaspoon red pepper flakes

1 tablespoon chopped fresh oregano or marjoram leaves

6 small-to-medium potatoes, not more than 2 1/2 inches long, peeled and cut into 1/8-inch-thick rounds or ovals

2 medium red onions, peeled and cut into 1/8-inch-thick rings

3 garlic cloves, peeled and cut into very thin slivers

12 whole basil leaves

3 medium zucchini, trimmed and cut into 1/8-inch-thick rounds

2 medium green bell peppers, seeded and cut into 1/4-inch-thick rings

6 ripe, firm plum tomatoes, cored and cut lengthwise into 1/8-inch-thick ovals

6 tablespoons crumbled Greek feta

Heat the grill to medium. Cut six 18 × 9-inch heavyweight aluminum foil rectangles and fold them in half lengthwise.

In a large bowl, whisk together the olive oil, mustard, salt, pepper, red pepper flakes, and oregano. Toss the potatoes, onions, and garlic in the marinade, and, using a slotted spoon so that as much of the marinade as possible drips back into the bowl, place equal amounts of potatoes and onions on the bottom center of each rectangle. Place one basil leaf on top. Toss the zucchini in the marinade and add in equal portions to the potatoes, as if building a small mound. Repeat with the bell peppers, place a basil leaf on top, and then repeat with the tomatoes so that they are at the top of the small mound. Sprinkle a tablespoon of crumbled feta on top of each.

Fold the packets to close them, joining the bottom and top edges to seal shut. Place in a shallow baking pan on a hot part of the grill, close the grill lid, and cook for about 35 minutes. Remove, place on individual plates, and serve.

GRILLED PEPPER BOATS WITH SPICY CHEESE

WE SERVE THIS at Pylos, a Greek restaurant in Manhattan's East Village, where I am consulting chef. It's one of the signature items on the menu.

MAKES 8 MEZE SERVINGS OR 4 HEARTIER PORTIONS

4 red, green, or yellow bell peppers, halved lengthwise and seeded, and 1 green and 1 red bell pepper, left whole

1/2 pound Greek feta

2 jalapeños, or more to taste

2 to 3 pickled peperoncini peppers, seeded and chopped

1 garlic clove, minced

1/4 to 1/3 cup extra virgin olive oil

Strained fresh juice of 1 lemon

2 to 6 tablespoons hot sauce, or to taste

Freshly ground black pepper to taste

Blanch the bell pepper halves in boiling salted water for 30 seconds to soften slightly. Remove with a slotted spoon, cool, and blot dry on paper towels.

Crumble the feta and set aside.

Heat the grill to medium. Place the whole green and red bell peppers and the jalapeños on the grill rack directly over the heat. Grill the bell peppers for about 20 minutes and the jalapeños for about 8 minutes, turning all of them once or twice, until the skins are charred and the peppers are soft. Remove, cool slightly, peel, and seed.

Pulse the pickled peppers and garlic in the bowl of a food processor. Add the feta and pulse to combine. Add the olive oil, lemon juice, hot sauce, and black pepper and keep pulsing until smooth.

Fill each pepper half with several tablespoons of the spicy cheese filling. For each pepper, fold a 24 × 18-inch piece of heavy aluminum foil in half to make an 18 × 12-inch rectangle. Place the filled pepper in the center of the foil and bring up the sides to cover the pepper, leaving a little space at the top. Fold the sides together to seal. Repeat with remaining peppers. Place the packets over direct heat on the grill for about 5 minutes. Remove, open carefully, and serve.

GREEK VEGETABLE KEBABS

THIS SIMPLE KEBAB can be eaten on its own as a main course with some grilled pita bread, or accompanied by a steaming plate of rice or small pasta, such as bowties or orzo.

MAKES 4 SERVINGS

Make the marinade: Combine the olive oil, lemon juice, garlic, herbs, salt, and pepper in a medium bowl. Toss the vegetables in the mixture and marinate for 1 to 6 hours.

Heat the grill to medium hot.

Remove and thread the vegetables onto the skewers, alternating the vegetables.

Place the skewers on the grill and cook, turning and brushing with the remaining marinade, for a total of about 12 minutes, or until the vegetables are tender and lightly charred. The oil in the marinade will likely flair up, so use a long-handled brush when doing this. Brush the pita with whatever remaining marinade there is and grill lightly. Remove and serve together.

For the marinade

½ cup extra virgin olive oil

Strained fresh juice of 1 large lemon

3 garlic cloves, minced

2 teaspoons dried oregano or savory

2 teaspoons dried mint

Salt and freshly ground black pepper to taste

1 large red bell pepper, cut into 1-inch squares

1 large green bell pepper, cut into 1-inch squares

3 long thin eggplants, cut into ½-inch rounds

2 medium zucchini, cut into ½-inch rounds

3 large red onions, cut into 1-inch squares

4 (12-inch) metal skewers

4 pita breads

GRILLED EGGPLANT LAYERED WITH TOMATOES AND FETA

THIS IS A SIMPLE, elegant dish that can be served as a light main course together with a salad or some pasta, or as a starter.

MAKES 6 SERVINGS

Vegetable oil for
brushing grill rack

3 medium eggplants, cut into
18 rounds about 1/2 inch thick

Olive oil for brushing vegetables,
plus 2 tablespoons for diluting
the pesto (optional)

3 medium-firm, ripe tomatoes,
cut into 4 rounds each

Salt and freshly ground
black pepper

12 large fresh basil leaves

12 (3-inch-square) slices of
feta, about 1/4 inch thick,
preferably the canned variety,
which is firmer, or 12 (1/2-inch)
slices of mozzarella

1/2 cup good-quality commercial
pesto (optional)

Heat the grill to medium. Brush the grill rack with a little oil.

Brush the eggplant slices on both sides with about 1/2 teaspoon of olive oil per side. Place on the grill, directly over the heat, and grill for about 6 minutes total, turning once with a spatula to cook on both sides. Remove and set aside.

Brush the tomato slices with olive oil and a little salt and pepper, and place on the grill carefully. Grill for 2 to 3 minutes per side. Remove and set aside. Turn off the grill.

Preheat the oven to 350°F (180°C). Oil the bottom and sides of six soufflé dishes or shallow baking dishes approximately 3 or 4 inches in diameter. Fill each terrine in the following order: eggplant slice, tomato slice, basil leaf, and feta slice. Repeat, and top with another eggplant slice. Press down lightly so the terrines aren't piled higher than the rims. Bake until the cheese melts, 12 to 15 minutes.

To serve, flip and turn out each terrine onto a medium plate. Drizzle with additional olive oil, if desired, or with pesto sauce diluted with a little olive oil.

GRILLED EGGPLANT WITH SMOKED TOMATO SAUCE AND YOGURT

MY FRIEND and colleague Leoni Stafyla first made this dish for me, grilling the eggplants under the broiler. It's a lovely dish for company and for Sunday lunch in the summer.

MAKES 6 SERVINGS

3 large eggplants, cut lengthwise into ¼-inch slices

Salt

1 cup extra virgin olive oil

1 medium onion, finely chopped

2 medium garlic cloves, finely chopped

1½ pounds firm, ripe tomatoes, cored and quartered

1 teaspoon sugar

2 tablespoons balsamic vinegar

Freshly ground black pepper to taste

2 tablespoons chopped fresh oregano or basil leaves

3 to 4 cups Greek-style strained yogurt

Place the eggplant slices in layers in a colander, salting between each layer, and place a plate and then several weights, such as cans, on top so that the bitter juices can drain. Leave the eggplant slices to drain for 30 to 40 minutes. Remove from the colander. Pat dry but do not rinse.

While the eggplants are draining, start the sauce: In a large, heavy skillet over medium heat, heat 2 tablespoons olive oil. Add the onion and sauté for 5 minutes, stirring. Add the garlic and stir all together for another minute or so. Reduce the heat to low and slowly cook the onion until it is light amber and slightly caramelized, about 15 minutes.

Heat the grill to medium hot.

Place the tomatoes in a shallow, lightly oiled baking pan and sprinkle with salt and the sugar. Using a pastry brush, dab each tomato section with a little of the balsamic vinegar. Close the lid on the grill (make sure the vents are open) and smoke the tomatoes until they are wilted and crusty, about 25 minutes. Remove and purée in a food processor. Pour the tomato purée into the onion-garlic mixture. Raise the heat and cook until the sauce comes to a boil, then reduce the heat to low. Add salt, pepper, and the herbs and cook the sauce for about 5 minutes. Remove from the heat.

Brush each eggplant slice with olive oil and grill until tender and lined with grill marks, about 6 minutes. Turn once to cook on both sides.

Strew a layer of eggplant slices over the surface of a rectangular serving dish (15 × 8 × 2½ inches). Spread a layer of sauce on top and then a layer of yogurt. Repeat until the ingredients are all used up, finishing with a layer of yogurt. Let the dish cool to room temperature and serve.

EGGPLANT ROLLS WITH CINNAMON-SCENTED TOMATO SAUCE

THE GREEK COOKS who emigrated from Turkey in the early part of the twentieth century brought their affection for the eggplant with them, together with myriad dishes that were unknown in Greece until then. This dish is a hybrid—part Greco-Turkish, part Italian. The sauce has decidedly Greek aromas, but the filling is less identifiable.

MAKES 4 SERVINGS

1 large eggplant, 1½ to 2 pounds

Salt

⅔ to 1 cup extra-virgin olive oil

1 medium red onion, finely chopped

1 garlic clove, minced

1½ pounds fresh plum tomatoes, grated or pulverized in a food processor (don't peel or seed them beforehand), or 2 cups canned chopped plum tomatoes

2 bay leaves

1 scant teaspoon sugar

1 cinnamon stick

2 allspice berries

Freshly ground black pepper to taste

2 tablespoons red wine vinegar

1 tablespoon chopped fresh oregano or 1 teaspoon dried Greek oregano

½ cup crumbled or mashed goat's milk cheese or Greek feta

½ cup grated ricotta salata or Greek manouri

½ cup grated Parmesan cheese

Trim the stem and blossom end off the eggplant and cut lengthwise into sixteen ¼-inch slices. Salt in layers in a colander and place a plate and then a weight, such as a heavy can, over the plate. Let stand for 30 to 40 minutes. Remove and pat dry, but do not rinse.

While the eggplants are draining, heat the grill to medium.

Heat 3 tablespoons olive oil over medium heat in a medium saucepan or large, deep skillet. Sauté the onion for 6 to 7 minutes, stirring, until soft, then add the garlic. Stir for a minute or so, then pour in the tomatoes. Bring to a boil, add the bay leaves, sugar, cinnamon stick, allspice, and salt and pepper. Reduce the heat and simmer, partially covered, until the sauce is thick, about 25 minutes. Stir in the vinegar, simmer for another 2 to 3 minutes, and add the oregano. Cook for another minute. Remove the spices and set the sauce aside.

Brush the eggplant slices generously with some of the remaining olive oil and grill over the hottest part of the grill, turning once and brushing again with oil, until the eggplant slices are tender but still firm and lined with grill marks. Remove and set aside to cool.

In a small bowl, combine the three cheeses and some pepper and mash with a fork. Lay the grilled eggplant strips vertically in front of you on a work surface or platter and place a heaping tablespoon of the cheese mixture on the bottom center of each. Roll up the eggplant slice to form a small cheese-filled cylinder and place seam side down on a clean platter. Repeat with the remaining cheese and the eggplant slices. Spoon the sauce over the eggplant rolls and serve.

GRILLED LATE SUMMER SQUASH WITH WALNUT-MINT PESTO

ACORN SQUASH and pumpkin both work nicely in this dish.

MAKES 6 SERVINGS

For the pesto

²/₃ cup coarsely ground walnuts

5 large garlic cloves

3 packed cups coarsely chopped mint leaves

¹/₂ cup extra virgin olive oil

²/₃ cup grated Parmesan cheese or crumbled firm Greek feta

Salt and freshly ground black pepper to taste

3 tablespoons fresh lemon juice, or more as needed

Vegetable oil for brushing grill rack

1 small acorn or butternut squash, about 3 pounds, or a 3-pound wedge of pumpkin, peeled and seeded

¹/₂ cup extra virgin olive oil

Salt and freshly ground black pepper

Mint sprigs for garnish (optional)

Make the pesto: In the bowl of a food processor, pulse together the walnuts and garlic until mealy, about 1 minute. Add the mint and pulse to combine. Add the olive oil and cheese, and pulse again to combine. Season with salt and pepper, drizzle in the lemon juice, and pulse. With the processor on, slowly drizzle in enough water to make the mixture as thick as porridge. Adjust the seasoning with additional salt, pepper, or lemon juice. Set aside.

Heat the grill to medium heat and oil the grill rack.

Cut the squash or pumpkin into ¼-inch slices and toss in a bowl together with the olive oil and salt and pepper. Place on a medium-hot part of the grill and grill until softened and lined, turning once, about 4 minutes per side.

Place the grilled squash or pumpkin on a serving platter and dot each piece with the sauce. Garnish, if desired, with a sprig or two of fresh mint.

GRILLED PORTOBELLO MUSHROOMS WITH PARSLEY, GARLIC, AND OLIVE OIL

THROUGHOUT THE MEDITERRANEAN, all sorts of mushrooms, wild and cultivated, find their way to the grill. A little olive oil, salt, pepper, and some herbs and there is an appetizer or main course in the making. Large chanterelles are excellent grilled. The recipe below calls for portobellos, unusually meaty and so hearty that coupled with a small salad, some bread, and maybe a wedge of cheese, they easily become a grilled main course.

MAKES 4 APPETIZER SERVINGS OR 2 MAIN-COURSE SERVINGS

4 large portobello mushrooms

2 garlic cloves

$2/3$ cup extra virgin olive oil

Juice of 1 large lemon

Sea salt and freshly ground black pepper to taste

Vegetable oil for brushing grill rack

1 tablespoon balsamic vinegar

$1/4$ cup finely chopped flat-leaf parsley

Trim the stems off the portobellos and reserve for another use. Crush one of the garlic cloves with the blade of a large knife. Whisk together $1/3$ cup olive oil, the lemon juice, and the crushed garlic. Season with salt and pepper. Marinate the portobellos for 30 minutes, turning them frequently. Remove and hold them over the bowl in which they were marinating to let any excess liquid drip off.

Heat the grill to medium-low. Lightly oil the grill rack.

Place the mushrooms cap up on the grill over the hottest part of the grill (direct heat), turning them once and brushing them with the marinade as they grill. Remove when the grill marks are visible and the mushrooms are lightly charred.

While the mushrooms are grilling, place the remaining $1/3$ cup olive oil, the balsamic vinegar, parsley, and remaining garlic clove in a food processor and pulse until smooth and emulsified. Season with salt and pepper and pulse to combine.

Slice the mushrooms on the diagonal, and spread each one fanlike on individual plates. Drizzle the olive oil and parsley mixture around them, sprinkle with pepper, and serve.

GRILLED ARTICHOKES WITH SMOKY SKORDALIA

GRILLED ARTICHOKES are one of the harbingers of spring. Greeks like to grill the thorny wild artichokes that come to farmers' markets in April, but the more common globes sold here will do just fine. Serve with a smoky skordalia, made with grilled potatoes, garlic, olive oil, and lemon juice.

MAKES 4 SERVINGS

1 lemon

4 large globe artichokes

4 tablespoons extra virgin olive oil

1 scant teaspoon sea salt

For the skordalia

3 large potatoes, peeled

$2/3$ cup extra virgin olive oil, or more as needed

Salt and freshly ground black pepper to taste

1 head garlic, halved

Strained fresh juice of 1 lemon, or more as needed

Fill a medium bowl with cold water and squeeze the lemon into it. Remove the toughest upper part of each artichoke with a serrated knife, cutting away at least 1 inch. Hold each artichoke round side down and trim away the tough outer leaves with the serrated knife, leaving the most tender, inner ones intact. Cut away all but $1/2$ inch of the stems. Cut the artichokes in half lengthwise so that the choke is exposed. Work fast to remove the choke with a spoon. Drop the artichokes into the acidulated water.

Bring a pot of salted water to a rolling boil and blanch the artichokes for 6 to 7 minutes. Remove with a slotted spoon, rinse under cold water, drain, and cool. Toss the artichokes with the 4 tablespoons olive oil and the sea salt. Set aside.

Begin the skordalia: Simmer the potatoes in the same water for about 20 minutes, until they can be pierced with a knife. Drain and set aside.

Heat the grill to medium. Have an 18 × 9-inch piece of aluminum foil ready.

Fold the foil in half along the long edge. Toss the hot, semi-boiled potatoes with $1/3$ cup olive oil and a little salt and pepper and place inside the aluminum foil. Fold over to form a package and seal the edges by turning up the bottom and top layers of foil inward. Wrap the garlic halves in another piece of aluminum foil. Place the potatoes and garlic on the grill and close the lid (make sure the vents are open). Smoke for 15 minutes. Remove.

When the potatoes are done, raise the heat or shuffle the coals and grill the artichokes on the hottest part of the grill for about 7 minutes, turning, so that the grill marks are visible on all sides and the artichokes tender.

Finish the skordalia: Place the potatoes and garlic in a mortar and pound to a paste with the pestle. Add salt as you go. Drizzle in the remaining $1/3$ cup olive oil and the lemon juice. The dip should be the consistency of mashed potatoes. Adjust the seasoning and consistency as you go with more salt, olive oil, and lemon juice, as needed. Remove the artichokes from the grill and serve with the dip.

SPANISH-STYLE GRILLED ARTICHOKES

GRILLED ARTICHOKES are found all over the Mediterranean, especially on the European side. I like this Spanish classic perhaps because it resembles the artichokes I know as a Greek cook, but it adds an ethnic twist—an unbridled dose of sherry vinegar.

MAKES 8 SERVINGS

1½ cups sherry vinegar

Strained fresh juice of 3 lemons

1 cup extra virgin olive oil

Salt and white pepper to taste

8 large globe artichokes

Whisk together the vinegar, lemon juice, olive oil, salt, and pepper. Trim the artichokes of their tough bottom leaves and cut off their stalks. Cut in half lengthwise. Using a teaspoon, scrape out their purple feathery chokes. Place the artichoke halves in a large bowl. Pour in the marinade. Cover and refrigerate for 8 hours or overnight. Bring to room temperature before grilling.

Heat the grill to medium-hot.

Drain the artichokes, pat dry, and reserve the marinade. Place the artichokes cut side down on the grill. Grill for 6 to 7 minutes, brushing with a little marinade. Turn and continue grilling another 5 to 6 minutes, brushing the cut sides with the marinade, too. The oil will flair up a little as you do this, so do it carefully, using a long-handled brush if necessary. Remove and serve immediately.

GRILLED SWEET POTATOES AND
LEEKS WITH MINT, ORANGE, AND OLIVE VINAIGRETTE

SWEET POTATOES and leeks are exceptional on the grill. This dish is filling and chock full of surprising flavors.

MAKES 4 SERVINGS

1 pound long sweet potatoes, scrubbed

3 large leeks, roots, tough upper greens, and outer layers removed

Vegetable oil for brushing grill rack

1/3 cup extra virgin olive oil

Salt and freshly ground black pepper to taste

For the dressing

1/4 cup strained fresh orange juice

2 tablespoons strained fresh lemon juice

1/2 cup extra virgin olive oil

1/2 teaspoon sugar

Salt to taste

1 scant teaspoon pink peppercorns, ground with your fingertips

1 tablespoon Dijon mustard

1/2 cup chopped fresh mint leaves

10 Kalamata olives, pitted and sliced crosswise

Place the sweet potatoes in a large pot of cold, salted water and bring to a boil. Reduce the heat to a simmer and cook the potatoes until they can be pierced with a knife, about 30 minutes.

While the potatoes are cooking, slit the leeks lengthwise without cutting all the way through and wash thoroughly under cold water, removing any sand from their interior layers. Pat dry.

Heat the grill to medium-hot and oil the grill rack.

Remove the sweet potatoes and place in a cold water bath or rinse under cold water in a colander. When the potatoes are cool enough to handle, peel them and cut into 1/4-inch rounds. Cut the leeks on the bias into 1-inch thick ovals. Gently toss the leeks and sweet potatoes in the olive oil and season with salt and pepper, being careful not to separate the leeks' layers. Place the leeks and then the sweet potatoes on the hottest part of the grill and grill, turning once, until the leeks are lightly charred and caramelized and the potatoes are tender and lined with grill marks. The leeks will take 10 to 12 minutes total; the sweet potatoes 6 to 8 minutes. Remove and place in a serving bowl or on a small platter.

Make the dressing: In a medium bowl, whisk together the orange and lemon juices. Drizzle in the olive oil, whisking vigorously to emulsify. Add the sugar, salt, pink peppercorns, and mustard. Stir in the mint and olives, and pour over the sweet potatoes and leeks. Toss gently and serve.

liquid
SMOKE

There are two ways to think about grilled soups. The first is from the point of view of a whole pot gurgling over hot coals on the grill rack, absorbing the flavor of smoke in its entirety. That would be more like hearth cooking on a barbecue. The second is to use the grill as a means to flavor one or two components of a soup, or perhaps all of them.

Because the flavor of smoke is so delicious, it's worthwhile turning on the grill to flavor one or two ingredients that will find their way into soup. Most of these recipes call for the cook to keep one leg in the kitchen and one on the deck, using the barbecue for grilling, say, chorizo to adorn a split pea soup or eggplant to bejewel a cool yogurt soup, but the stovetop for finishing off the rest.

Grilled vegetables lend themselves especially well to soups. The Cold Yogurt Soup with Spicy Grilled Eggplant, with its sweet-sour pomegranate syrup, is a great balancing act of flavors and textures. Other soups are earthier, like the Grilled Mushroom and Garlic Soup and the Split-Pea Soup with Grilled Chorizo. Both could easily be adapted to indoor grills or even the broiler. One of my favorite soups among the handful that follows is the Grilled Vegetable Gazpacho. It speaks to my innate sense of economy as a home cook reared in Mediterranean tradition: You can easily turn leftover grilled vegetables into soup.

Vegetables for soup that work best on the grill because their flavors intensify and sweeten are tomatoes, onions, peppers, and eggplants—the quartet of vegetables that finds its way into countless summertime dishes all over the Mediterranean. Mushrooms and the grill are natural partners, too.

GRILLED TOMATO SOUP WITH SPICY YOGURT

THIS IS THE PERFECT soup for vegetable gardeners. Pick the tomatoes fresh if you can, throw them on the grill until pleasantly charred, and purée them with other ingredients in a food processor. The spicy yogurt is a lovely foil to the sweet ripe flavor of grilled seasonal tomatoes.

MAKE 4 TO 6 SERVINGS

Vegetable oil for
brushing grill rack

4 pounds firm ripe tomatoes

6 to 8 tablespoons extra virgin
olive oil, or more as needed

4 tablespoons balsamic
vinegar or strained fresh
lemon juice, or more to taste

2 teaspoons sugar

Salt and freshly ground black
pepper to taste

1 head garlic

1 long green chili pepper or
really hot sauce to taste

2 to 4 cups good-quality
chicken broth

1 cup Greek-style
strained yogurt

Zest of 1/2 lemon

2 scallions, white parts only,
very finely chopped

8 basil leaves, very
finely chopped

Heat the grill to medium and lightly oil the grill rack.

Wash and pat dry the tomatoes. Cut in half lengthwise and core. Toss the tomatoes with the olive oil, balsamic vinegar, sugar, and salt and pepper. Place the tomatoes on the grill rack. Wrap the garlic in foil and place on the rack, in the center of the tomatoes. Place the chili pepper, if using, in a corner of the grill rack. Cover the grill and smoke the tomatoes until they are fairly charred and caramelized, 12 to 15 minutes. Remove to a bowl. Remove the garlic head and the chili pepper.

Squeeze out the pulp from the garlic. Place in a food processor together with the tomatoes, in batches if necessary, and pulse on and off until the tomatoes are pulverized. Place the mixture in a large pot. Dilute to desired consistency with the broth and heat. Add a little olive oil if necessary to make the consistency of the soup a little more velvety. Adjust the flavor with additional salt, pepper, and vinegar.

Peel and seed the chili pepper. Combine the yogurt, lemon zest, and chili pepper in a small bowl. Serve the soup in individual bowls. Sprinkle with chopped scallions and sprinkle the basil over the surface of the soup. Spoon a dollop of the yogurt mixture in the center or mix it in and serve.

GRILLED VEGETABLE GAZPACHO

I MAKE TWO VERSIONS of this soup, both more or less inspired by leftovers. The first is a gazpacho culled from a Greek summer salad and the second is this, a version of gazpacho that calls for grilled, instead of fresh, vegetables. This is a lovely accompaniment to grilled pizzas, meats, and even fish.

MAKES 6 SERVINGS

2 red bell peppers

2 yellow bell peppers

1 long green fresh chili pepper, seeded and split in half lengthwise (optional)

2 large red onions, quartered

1 pound medium zucchini, cut lengthwise into ¼-inch-thick slices

2½ pounds large, firm, vine-ripened tomatoes, cored, halved, and seeded

½ cup extra virgin olive oil, or more as needed

Salt and freshly ground black pepper to taste

3 large garlic cloves

½ cup chopped fresh basil

¼ cup chopped fresh oregano

2 tablespoons red wine vinegar or lime juice, or more to taste

Heat the grill to medium-hot.

Place the bell peppers, chili pepper, onions, zucchini, and tomatoes in a large stainless steel or glass bowl and toss with the olive oil and a little salt and pepper. Place the vegetables on the grill, in batches if necessary, starting with the peppers and onions, which take the longest, 10 to 12 minutes. Next, place the tomatoes, then the zucchini on the grill, 8 to 10 and 6 to 8 minutes respectively. Grill until the zucchini are soft and lined with grill marks, the peppers are soft and charred, the onions lightly charred and softened, and the tomatoes softened and browned along the edges and wrinkled. The grilling time for each vegetable will vary slightly, but overall the whole batch should take 30 to 35 minutes to grill.

Remove the peppers to a separate bowl and cover with plastic wrap. Let cool for about 10 minutes, then peel and seed, reserving their juices.

Coarsely chop all the vegetables. Place in a food processor together with the garlic, basil, oregano, and 1 cup of cold water. Purée at high speed until totally pulverized and smooth. Add more water if necessary to reach a velvety consistency. Strain, if desired, through a fine-mesh sieve. Place the vegetable mixture in a container in the refrigerator and let cool for about 2 hours before serving. Adjust the seasoning with additional salt and pepper to taste and mix in the vinegar just before serving.

GRILLED EGGPLANT SOUP

THIS SOUP, SATING and elegant, is a perfect first course before grilled meat, fish, or poultry. I serve it with the Grilled Pepper Boats with Spicy Cheese (page 24) and a salad, or with a grilled burger or simple marinated chicken.

MAKES 4 SERVINGS

Vegetable oil for
brushing grill rack

2 large eggplants (about
3 pounds), peeled and cut
lengthwise into $1/2$-inch slices

1 tablespoon chopped
fresh thyme, plus additional
for garnish

1 tablespoon chopped
fresh oregano leaves

3 garlic cloves, minced

$1/2$ cup extra virgin olive oil

2 tablespoons balsamic vinegar

2 large red onions,
finely chopped

5 cups chicken or
vegetable stock

Salt and freshly ground
black pepper to taste

Greek-style strained yogurt
or sour cream for garnish

Heat the grill to medium and oil the grill rack.

In a large bowl, toss the eggplant slices with the thyme, oregano, half the garlic, $1/4$ cup olive oil, and the balsamic vinegar. Grill, turning, until soft and lined, 6 to 8 minutes. Set aside.

In a large pot, heat the remaining $1/4$ cup olive oil over medium heat and sauté the onions until soft, about 10 minutes. Add the remaining garlic and stir for a minute or so. Pour in the stock and add the grilled eggplant. Simmer for 20 minutes. Using an immersion blender, purée the soup in the pot or strain it and purée in batches in a food processor. Pour the purée back into the soup, add salt and pepper, and heat through. To serve, place in bowls and top with yogurt and fresh thyme.

COLD YOGURT SOUP WITH SPICY GRILLED EGGPLANT

FEW MEDITERRANEAN dishes are as refreshing and filling as cold yogurt soup. The grilled eggplant flavored with pomegranate syrup is a classic duet in certain parts of the eastern Mediterranean. In the variation, with zucchini, the pomegranate syrup is replaced with hot pepper oil and the resulting soup changes from tart and sweet to hot and cool.

MAKES 6 SERVINGS

1 medium eggplant, about
1½ pounds, cut lengthwise
into ¼-inch slices

5 cups Greek- or
Mediterranean-style
strained yogurt

3 garlic cloves

⅔ cup fresh mint
leaves, chopped

Salt and freshly ground
black pepper to taste

2 to 2½ cups ice water

⅔ cup pomegranate syrup

Vegetable oil for
brushing grill rack

½ cup olive oil, or
more as needed

½ teaspoon cayenne pepper

3 tablespoons balsamic vinegar

3 tablespoons pomegranate
seeds for garnish

Place the eggplant slices in layers in a colander, salting between each layer. Place a plate or paper towels on top and a weight on top to facilitate the draining. Let the eggplant stand for 30 to 40 minutes. Remove, pat dry with paper towels, but do not rinse.

Place the yogurt, 1 garlic clove, the mint, salt, pepper, and the ice water in a food processor or blender and purée at high speed to pulverize the mint and garlic. Transfer to a serving bowl, cover with plastic wrap, and place in the refrigerator to chill. Using a mortar and pestle, pound the remaining 2 garlic cloves with a little salt until they form a paste. Add the pomegranate syrup and mix well. Set aside.

Heat the grill to medium and brush the rack with oil.

In a medium bowl, whisk together the olive oil, cayenne, and vinegar and toss the eggplant slices in the mixture. Grill over a medium-hot part of the grill until soft, about 8 minutes total, turning once or twice and brushing with the olive oil mixture. Do this carefully, as the oil may flare up on the grill. Remove, cool slightly, and cut into ½-inch dice. Toss the eggplant with the pomegranate mixture. Divide into six equal portions. Ladle the soup into individual bowls, add the pomegranate-flavored grilled eggplant, and drizzle in a little more olive oil if desired. Garnish each bowl with ½ tablespoon pomegranate seeds and serve immediately.

Cold Yogurt Soup with Grilled Zucchini and Red Pepper Oil

For the pepper oil, heat $1/2$ cup extra virgin olive oil over medium heat just to warm and add 1 heaping teaspoon red pepper flakes. Set aside. (It's best to do this at least a day ahead of time so that the oil can absorb some of the pepper flakes' heat.) For six servings, cut 2 medium zucchini lengthwise into $1/4$-inch slices and toss, as with the eggplant, in the olive oil and vinegar, omitting the cayenne in the mixture. Grill over medium heat until soft and lined with grill marks, and cut into $1/2$-inch dice. Serve the chilled yogurt soup with equal amounts of the grilled zucchini and drizzle on the red pepper oil.

GRILLED MUSHROOM AND GARLIC SOUP

NOTHING SHORT of steak is quite as satisfying as mushrooms cooked on the grill. This variation on a classic French cream of mushroom soup is replete with delicate tarragon and thyme.

MAKES 6 SERVINGS

1 head garlic

3 large red or yellow onions, peeled and quartered

²/₃ cup extra virgin olive oil

8 medium-large portobello mushrooms

2 tablespoons unsalted butter

Salt and freshly ground black pepper to taste

2 teaspoons dried tarragon

2 teaspoons dried marjoram or thyme

2 tablespoons all-purpose flour

1 cup dry white wine

1¼ quarts chicken or vegetable stock

³/₄ cup heavy cream

1 tablespoon balsamic vinegar

Heat the grill to medium.

Wrap the garlic head in aluminum foil and place on the grill. Close the lid, leaving the vents open, and smoke the garlic for about 20 minutes.

In a medium bowl, toss the onions with 3 tablespoons of the olive oil. Brush the remaining oil generously over the portobellos. Open the grill cover. Place the onion quarters and mushrooms on the grill. Turn several times, for a total of 12 to 15 minutes, until the mushrooms are soft and wrinkled and the onions are slightly charred. Remove, cool slightly, and chop.

Remove the garlic. Open the aluminum foil and let the garlic cool until it can be handled.

In a large pot over medium heat, melt the butter. Add the chopped onions and sauté until glossy and totally wilted, about 8 minutes. Add the mushrooms and garlic, and toss to coat. Sprinkle with salt and pepper, tarragon, and marjoram. Sprinkle in the flour and turn until the mixture becomes a little pasty. Pour in the wine. As soon as the alcohol evaporates, add the stock. Bring to a boil over high heat, reduce the heat to medium, and simmer for 15 minutes for the flavors to meld. Remove from the heat. With an immersion blender, purée the soup in the pot. Alternatively, let it cool slightly, drain it, reserve the liquid, and purée the solids to a creamy consistency in a food processor at high speed. Place the purée back in the pot and stir over medium heat. Add the cream and stir. Add the vinegar, stir well, adjust the seasoning with salt and pepper, and serve.

GREEK-INSPIRED GRILLED LETTUCE AND LAMB SOUP

THIS DISH is a take on the traditional Greek Easter soup, *magei-ritsa*. It was inspired by a deconstructed version I tasted by chef Michael Psilakis of Onera Restaurant in New York City. The grilled lettuce is a real surprise because that familiar, milky quality that lettuce has is completely transformed into something else, deep and earthy, a crisp flavor despite the soft, wilted texture of the grilled leaves.

MAKES 8 SERVINGS

Vegetable oil for brushing grill rack

For the lamb

2 pounds boneless, butterflied leg of lamb (bone reserved)

3 garlic cloves, cut in half

Salt and freshly ground black pepper to taste

3 tablespoons extra virgin olive oil

2 teaspoons ground fennel seeds

2 teaspoons dried oregano

2 teaspoons ground dried rosemary

For the grilled vegetables

1 medium fennel bulb, trimmed and quartered

1 medium leek, trimmed and washed thoroughly, cut into 2-inch-long cylinders

Heat the grill to hot and brush the grill rack with oil.

Prepare the lamb: Rub the lamb with the cut side of the garlic and discard the garlic. Season the lamb generously all over with salt and pepper. Combine the olive oil and herbs in a small bowl and rub the mixture all over the lamb. Place the lamb on the grill and cook for 15 to 20 minutes for rare (it will cook a little more inside the soup). Turn occasionally as you grill. Remove and set aside.

Prepare the vegetables: Wash and pat dry the fennel, leek, scallions, garlic, and romaine lettuce. In a large bowl, toss the fennel, leek, scallions, and garlic with the olive oil, red pepper flakes, and salt and pepper. Place on the grill and cook, turning occasionally, until soft and lined with grill marks, 10 to 12 minutes. Remove and set aside. Toss the romaine leaves in the same bowl, replenishing the olive oil, salt, and pepper if necessary. Grill the leaves until wilted, about 5 minutes, turning. Remove. Coarsely chop the vegetables.

Make the soup: Heat the olive oil in a large pot and add the lamb bone. Sear over high heat. Add the chopped grilled vegetables and the rice, and toss all together to coat in the oil. Pour in the stock and bring to a boil over high heat. Simmer for 30 to 40 minutes, skimming the foam off the top. Season with salt and pepper. Remove the vegetables and rice with a slotted spoon and transfer to the bowl of a food processor. Purée at high

6 scallions, trimmed

2 heads fresh green garlic,
with stalks

1 large head romaine lettuce
(about 1 pound), root end
removed, leaves separated

$\frac{1}{2}$ cup extra virgin olive oil,
or more as needed

1 teaspoon red pepper flakes

Salt and freshly ground
black pepper to taste

For the soup

4 tablespoons olive oil

1 lamb bone, from
the leg or shank

$\frac{1}{2}$ cup long-grain rice

2 quarts chicken stock or
water, or more as needed

Salt and freshly ground
black pepper to taste

$\frac{1}{2}$ cup finely chopped fresh dill

Juice of 1 to 2 lemons, to taste

speed. Remove the lamb bone from the soup and discard. Pour the pu-réed vegetables back into the soup. Cut the grilled lamb into thin strips, and place in the soup. Add the chopped dill. Heat for a few minutes to warm through, then thin the soup to the desired consistency with water or stock. Pour in half the lemon juice, adjust the seasoning with salt and pepper and lemon juice, and serve.

SPLIT PEA SOUP WITH GRILLED CHORIZO

THIS SPANISH-STYLE dish, with its wintry feel, is lovely in the fall. Split peas and sausage are natural partners. Substitute the chorizo with any sausage of choice, such as Italian fennel-flavored sausages.

MAKES 6 TO 8 SERVINGS

1/2 cup extra virgin olive oil

2 medium yellow onions, finely chopped

2 medium green bell peppers, seeded and finely chopped

2 medium waxy potatoes, peeled and cut into 1/4-inch cubes

2 garlic cloves, minced

2 cups dried green or yellow split peas, sorted and washed

2 quarts water or chicken stock, or more as needed

2 bay leaves

Salt and freshly ground black pepper to taste

3/4 pound chorizo, cut into 1/4-inch rounds

2 to 3 tablespoons Spanish sherry vinegar

Paprika for garnish

In a large Dutch oven or pot, heat the olive oil over medium heat and sauté the onions and peppers until soft, about 10 minutes. Add the potatoes and toss to coat in the oil. Cook, stirring, for 3 to 4 minutes. Add the garlic and toss to coat. Add the split peas and toss.

Pour in the water or stock. Raise the heat to high and bring to a boil. Reduce the heat to medium, add the bay leaves, and simmer the soup for 1 1/2 to 2 hours, until the peas have disintegrated. Season with salt and pepper during the last half hour of cooking.

Heat the grill to medium-hot.

Place the chorizo slices on the grill, and turn once or twice until cooked through and lined with grill marks, 5 to 6 minutes total. Remove.

Remove the bay leaves from the soup. Using an immersion blender, purée the soup in the pot. (You can also do this in a food processor by straining the soup and puréeing it hot, in batches, at high speed in a food processor. Place back in the pot.) Stir in the sherry vinegar. Serve the soup in individual bowls topped with several slices of grilled chorizo and a sprinkling of paprika.

BREADY

things on the grill

My first taste of a real grilled Mediterranean sandwich is not something I associate with outdoor cooking at all but with a food fad in Athens in the early 1980s called *tost*. Tost was, after the spit-roasted gyro, Athens' first real fast food and an instant hit with teenagers. Served out of tiny shops, tost was a kind of potpourri sandwich. At the front of each shop, in a tip of the hat to old Greek tavernas with their open kitchens and exposed pots, small tubs of raw ingredients were lined up all in a row: ham, salami, cheeses, tomatoes, boiled eggs, hot dogs, and various spicy and tangy spreads. Once the customer chose the fillings, the person behind the counter stuffed everything inside an oblong roll and then placed it on a ridged iron hot plate that clamped down so that the tost was grilled on both sides.

No doubt, the recipes that follow are a bit more high brow! That notwithstanding, bready things on the grill are by nature fast, easy, casual, and fun. With the exception of the grilled pizzas, which need proofing time for the dough, these are all recipes you could make on almost a moment's notice.

Some recipes, such as bruschetta, are obviously meant as light starters or snacks. Pizza, as well as most panini and sandwiches, could easily be main courses, especially for lunch or an early dinner and especially if accompanied by a grilled salad or grilled vegetable dish.

Since bready things on the grill are mostly quick and easy to make, the grill may be used for a whole range of other foods, too, such as pasta dishes, soups, and of course desserts.

GRILLED GREEK PIZZA WITH ONIONS, OLIVES, AND FETA CHEESE

THIS IS A FAVORITE summer dish on our barbecue. I make a simple homemade tomato sauce by sautéing a finely chopped medium red onion and three chopped garlic cloves in $1/2$ cup of olive oil and then adding two cans of good-quality chopped tomatoes. The only seasoning is salt and a pinch of sugar. I let the sauce simmer for about an hour, until it thickens. Simple tomato sauces on pizza allow other ingredients to take the limelight.

MAKES 4 TO 6 SERVINGS

For the pizza dough

1 packet active dry yeast

$3/4$ cup warm water

$1/2$ teaspoon sugar

2 cups all-purpose flour, plus $1/2$ to 1 cup for adding during kneading

$1/3$ cup extra virgin olive oil, plus 2 teaspoons for brushing on dough

$1/2$ teaspoon salt

3 tablespoons coarsely ground cornmeal, or more as needed

Make the dough: In a large bowl, combine the yeast, water, and sugar and mix with a fork. Cover with plastic wrap and let stand in a warm place for 10 minutes, or until the starter begins to foam. Add the flour, $1/3$ cup olive oil, and the salt and mix with a wooden spoon until a dough mass forms. Knead in the bowl, sprinkling with a little additional flour, until the bowl is clean and the dough smooth and elastic, about 10 minutes. (You may also do this in the bowl of an electric mixer with a dough hook, at medium speed for 5 to 7 minutes.) Place the dough in an oiled bowl, cover with plastic wrap, and let stand for 1 to 2 hours in a warm place, until doubled in bulk.

Heat the grill to medium high. If using a traditional charcoal grill, arrange the charcoal around the perimeter, leaving enough room for at least one 10-inch round pizza to fit in the center. If using gas, the heat is easier to adjust.

Divide the dough in half using a sharp knife and on a lightly floured surface roll out each half into a 10-inch circle. Brush each side of the rounds with a teaspoon olive oil. Sprinkle with cornmeal, flipping so that both sides are sprinkled. Place one round at a time on the grill and grill the dough, turning once, for a total of 6 to 8 minutes. Repeat with second round. The rounds should be fairly firm and lined with grill marks when they are done. Remove and set aside for a few minutes.

For the topping

1 cup good-quality commercial or homemade tomato sauce

1 cup chopped pitted Kalamata olives

6 small pickled pepperoncini peppers, seeded and cut into thin slices

2 medium onions, peeled, halved, and cut into $\frac{1}{8}$-inch-thick slices

6 ounces Greek feta, crumbled

2 tablespoons chopped fresh oregano

3 tablespoons extra virgin olive oil for drizzling over pizzas

Make the topping: Spread half the tomato sauce over each of the pizza rounds. Top each with half the olives, half the pepperoncini, half the onions, and half the feta. Sprinkle each with 1 tablespoon oregano and drizzle with $1\frac{1}{2}$ tablespoons olive oil.

Carefully slide one round onto the center of the grill, over indirect heat or over the least hot part of the grill. Cover and bake for 7 to 8 minutes, or until the cheese is melted and the topping hot. Remove, serve, and repeat with the remaining pizza round.

GRILLED WHOLE WHEAT PIZZA WITH RED PEPPERS, GOAT CHEESE, AND BASIL

THIS RECIPE WORKS WELL with any soft, mildly sharp cheese that turns creamy when melted.

MAKES 4 SERVINGS

For the pizza dough

1 packet active dry yeast

³/₄ cup warm water

¹/₂ teaspoon sugar

1¹/₂ cups all-purpose flour, plus ¹/₂ to ³/₄ cup for kneading

¹/₂ cup whole wheat flour

¹/₃ cup extra virgin olive oil

¹/₂ teaspoon salt

Make the dough: In a large bowl, combine the yeast, water, and sugar and mix with a fork. Cover with plastic wrap and let stand in a warm place for 10 minutes, or until the starter begins to foam. Add the flours, olive oil, and salt and mix with a wooden spoon until a dough mass forms. Knead in the bowl, sprinkling with a little additional flour, until the bowl is clean and the dough smooth and elastic, about 10 minutes. (You may also do this in the bowl of an electric mixer with a dough hook, at medium speed for 5 to 7 minutes.) Place the dough in an oiled bowl, cover with plastic wrap, and let stand for about 1 hour in a warm place, until doubled in bulk.

Heat the grill to medium. The pizza has to be grilled on the least hot part of the grill. If using a traditional charcoal grill, arrange the charcoal around the perimeter, leaving enough room for at least one 10-inch round pizza to fit in the center. If using gas, the heat is easier to adjust.

For the topping

3 red bell peppers

1 cup good-quality commercial or homemade tomato sauce

2 tablespoons extra virgin olive oil for brushing dough

2 to 3 tablespoons coarsely ground cornmeal

4 ounces speck, prosciutto, or Serrano ham, chopped

8 ounces soft goat cheese, cut into $1/2$ teaspoon dabs

3 tablespoons chopped fresh basil

1 teaspoon red pepper flakes

Salt to taste

3 tablespoons extra virgin olive oil for drizzling over pizzas

Make the topping: Grill the peppers on the hottest part of the grill or, if using traditional charcoal, along the edges of the grill, directly over the coals, for 5 to 6 minutes, turning to char on all sides. Remove to a bowl and cover with plastic wrap. When the peppers are cool enough to handle, peel them and split them lengthwise down the center to remove the seeds and stems. Chop and set aside. Pour the juice from the peppers into a small bowl and empty the tomato sauce into that. Mix.

Divide the dough in half using a sharp knife, and on a lightly floured surface roll out each half into a 10-inch circle. Brush each side of the rounds with olive oil. Sprinkle with cornmeal, flipping so that both sides are sprinkled. Place one round at a time on the grill and grill the dough, turning once, for a total of 6 to 8 minutes. Repeat with the second round. The rounds should be fairly firm and lined with grill marks when they are done. Remove and set aside for a few minutes.

Spread each pizza round with half the pepper-tomato sauce and sprinkle with half the grilled peppers and half the cured ham, goat cheese, basil, red pepper flakes, and salt. Drizzle each pizza with $1^1/2$ tablespoons of olive oil. Carefully slide one round onto the center of the grill, over indirect heat. Cover and bake for 7 to 8 minutes, or until the cheese is melted and the topping hot. Remove, serve, and repeat with the remaining pizza round.

SPICY FETA AND RED PEPPER BRUSCHETTA

GRILLED OR ROASTED red peppers and feta are a duet that takes many different forms in Greece; it appears as a filling for stuffed peppers and certain meat dishes, as a dip with chips, and as a spread, as in the following recipe.

MAKES 12 SERVINGS

2 large red bell peppers

$\frac{1}{2}$ cup extra virgin olive oil, plus a little more for drizzling over bread

Salt

3 tablespoons coarsely chopped fresh oregano leaves

$\frac{1}{2}$ pound Greek feta

Tabasco or other hot pepper sauce to taste

$\frac{1}{2}$ to 1 teaspoon freshly ground black pepper

1 tablespoon fresh lemon juice

1 baguette, cut on the diagonal into 12 ($\frac{1}{3}$-inch-thick) slices

Heat the grill to medium.

Place the red peppers on the grill, turning, for 10 to 14 minutes total, until charred on all sides. Remove, place in a shallow bowl, and cover with plastic wrap. When the peppers are cool enough to handle, peel and seed in the bowl. Strain the juices and set aside. Cut the peppers lengthwise into strips about $\frac{1}{8}$ inch thick. Toss with 1 tablespoon olive oil, a little salt, and 1 tablespoon oregano.

Combine the feta, $\frac{1}{4}$ cup olive oil, Tabasco, pepper juices, black pepper, and lemon juice in a food processor and pulse on and off until smooth and spreadable. Set aside.

Brush the bread slices on both sides with the remaining olive oil. Grill for about 2 minutes per side. Remove.

Spread each piece of grilled bread with about 1 heaping tablespoon of the whipped spicy feta. Top with a few strips of roasted red pepper and sprinkle with the remaining oregano. Drizzle with a little extra virgin olive oil and serve.

BRUSCHETTA WITH PESTO-FLAVORED MUSHROOMS

MUSHROOMS TOSSED with pesto are an Italian classic, revisited here as a topping for Mediterranean-style grilled bread. This makes a lovely starter to an elegant meal.

MAKES 12 SERVINGS

½ cup olive oil

1 pound button mushrooms, trimmed and chopped

1 garlic clove, peeled and chopped

2 tablespoons good-quality commercial pesto

½ to 1 scant teaspoon hot pepper flakes

Salt to taste

1 baguette, cut on the diagonal into 12 (½-inch-thick) slices

¼ cup finely chopped fresh flat-leaf parsley

Freshly ground black pepper to taste

Heat the grill to medium.

Heat 2 tablespoons of the olive oil in a large, heavy skillet over medium-high heat and sauté the mushrooms for 3 minutes. (If you have a heavy skillet with a heatproof handle, you can do this on the grill.) Add the garlic, stir, and continue sautéing for another 2 to 3 minutes, until most of the pan juices have evaporated. Remove from the heat and mix in the pesto, 2 tablespoons olive oil, the hot pepper flakes, and salt. Set aside.

Brush the bread on both sides with the remaining olive oil and grill for about 2 minutes per side. Remove. Spoon a little of the mushroom mixture over each slice of bread, sprinkle with parsley and pepper, and serve.

GRILLED HALOUMI AND RAISIN BREAD SANDWICHES WITH OUZO-FIRED GRAPES

WE SERVE THIS as a meze at Pylos, a Greek restaurant in New York's East Village, where I am consulting chef. Haloumi is a Cypriot cheese that works great on the grill because it softens but doesn't melt.

MAKES 4 SERVINGS

12 (1/2-inch-thick) slices
raisin-walnut, walnut, or
whole wheat bread

8 (1/4-inch-thick) slices haloumi
cheese (about 1 pound)

6 tablespoons (3/4 stick)
unsalted butter, softened

4 tablespoons pine nuts

1 1/2 cups seedless red
grapes, halved

1/2 cup anise-flavored liqueur,
such as ouzo or Sambucca

2 tablespoons chopped
fresh mint

Heat the grill to medium.

Remove the crusts from the bread and cut each slice to the same size as the haloumi slices. Spread 1/2 teaspoon of the softened butter on both sides of each slice of bread. Grill the bread lightly on both sides for 2 to 3 minutes total. Place the haloumi on the grill, too, and grill it on both sides until it begins to melt, about 5 minutes, turning once.

Remove the cheese and bread slices and assemble the sandwiches. Place one slice of haloumi on a slice of toasted bread, place a piece of bread on top, and repeat to make a double-decker sandwich. Set aside for a few minutes.

Place a cast-iron or nonstick skillet with a flameproof handle on the grill. Have your serving plates ready and nearby. Brown the pine nuts in the dry skillet for 2 to 3 minutes, shaking the pan back and forth to avoid burning the nuts. Add the remaining butter. When it melts, add the grapes and liqueur carefully, with your face and head away from the grill in case the liqueur flames up. Cook on the grill for 4 to 5 minutes, until the alcohol cooks off. Toss in the mint.

Place the sandwiches back on the grill for a few seconds, just to warm through. Place one sandwich in the center of each plate, cutting in half diagonally if desired, and pour the liqueur-grape mixture on top. Serve immediately.

GRILLED CYPRIOT HALOUMI CHEESE AND TOMATOES ON PITA BREAD

THIS SIMPLE APPETIZER can be made with almost any semi-hard mild cheese. The cheese needs to be hard enough so as not to melt, but mild enough so that it does not dehydrate on the grill and become overwhelmingly salty.

MAKES 6 SERVINGS

Vegetable oil for
brushing grill rack

3 large, firm ripe tomatoes

1/4 cup extra virgin olive oil, plus
more for garnish

Dash of sugar

Salt and freshly ground black
pepper to taste

2 teaspoons balsamic vinegar

10 ounces haloumi cheese,
cut into 1/4-inch slices

3 pita breads

3 tablespoons chopped fresh
flat-leaf parsley or basil

Heat the grill to medium-hot. Brush the rack lightly with oil.

Core the tomatoes and cut each into four wedges. Scoop out the seeds. In a small bowl, combine the olive oil, sugar, salt, pepper, and vinegar, and toss the tomatoes in the mixture. Grill, turning once, until the grill marks are visible and the tomatoes softened and beginning to blister.

Place the cheese slices on the rack and grill, turning once, until grill marks are visible and the cheese just begins to soften and color a little. Grill the pita bread to warm it through.

To serve, cut each pita bread into six triangular wedges and place three wedges on each plate. Add two tomato wedges and one piece of grilled haloumi. Drizzle with a little olive oil and sprinkle with chopped parsley. Serve immediately.

GRILLED EGGPLANT SANDWICHES WITH YOGURT-TAHINI-CHIPOTLE DRESSING

CHIPOTLE PEPPERS aren't a traditional variety in the Mediterranean, but this dish was born out of my work in the kitchen at New York's Pylos, where the chef, Juan Tzitzimititla, sometimes throws together what I like to call Mex-Med treats for himself and his Mexican cooks. Munch on this simple sandwich at lunchtime with a tall, cold beer.

MAKES 4 SERVINGS

1 medium eggplant
(about 1 pound)

Salt

For the tahini–chipotle
dressing

2 red bell peppers

1 cup Greek-style strained
yogurt

$1/3$ cup tahini

$1/4$ cup chopped chipotle
peppers, or more to taste

2 tablespoons fresh thyme

3 to 4 tablespoons fresh
lemon juice, to taste

Salt and freshly ground
black pepper to taste

$1/2$ cup extra virgin olive oil

4 pita breads

1 small bunch arugula,
trimmed and torn

1 large red onion, halved
and thinly sliced

Cut the eggplant into $1/8$-inch rounds. Layer and salt in a colander, place a weight, such as a plate and several cans, on top, and let drain for 30 minutes. Remove and pat dry the eggplant slices.

Heat the grill to medium.

Make the dressing: Grill the bell peppers over medium-high heat, turning, until the skins are charred and the flesh is soft, 10 to 12 minutes. Let cool slightly. Peel and seed the peppers and place in the bowl of a food processor. Pulse on and off to purée. Add the yogurt, tahini, chipotle peppers, thyme, lemon juice, and salt and pepper. Purée at high speed. Add between $1/3$ and $2/3$ cup water, as needed, to adjust the consistency of the dressing, which should be as dense as a thick batter. Set aside.

Place the olive oil in a medium bowl and toss in the eggplant slices. Grill over medium heat, flip once, and remove when the slices are tender but not so soft that they disintegrate, 3 to 4 minutes per side. Brush the pita breads with the remaining oil and grill slightly to brown lightly.

Spread about 1 tablespoon of the dressing over each pita. Top with the grilled eggplant, arugula, and onion. Roll up and secure closed with a toothpick. Pour the remaining dressing into each pita roll. Wrap the bottoms if desired with waxed paper or aluminum foil, and serve immediately, with plenty of napkins!

GRILLED PANINI WITH ONIONS, ARUGULA, BASIL, MOZZARELLA, AND BRESAOLA

I LOVE grilled sandwiches in any form, and all the better if they are stuffed with the Mediterranean's best offerings.

MAKES 4 SERVINGS

½ cup extra virgin olive oil

1 medium onion, cut in half lengthwise and then into thin slices

3 tablespoons balsamic vinegar

2 tablespoons fresh orange juice

1 large garlic clove, minced

Salt and freshly ground black pepper to taste

1 (1-pound) loaf fresh Italian or French bread or ciabatta

½ pound bresaola, prosciutto, or Serrano ham, cut into very thin slices

12 ounces fresh whole-milk mozzarella, thinly sliced

12 arugula leaves, trimmed and torn

12 large fresh basil leaves

2 ripe, firm tomatoes, cut into 12 rounds

Heat the grill to medium.

Have a heavy, preferably cast-iron, skillet with a flameproof handle ready. Heat ¼ cup of the olive oil in it on the grill. Add the onion. As soon as they start to sizzle, reduce the heat to very low, cover the skillet, and cook the onion until soft and lightly browned, about 15 minutes. Add 1 teaspoon balsamic vinegar to the skillet, stir, and cook another few minutes until the onion is lightly caramelized. Remove and cool slightly. (You can do this on your stovetop, too.)

Whisk together the remaining ¼ cup olive oil, remaining balsamic vinegar, orange juice, and garlic. Season lightly with salt and pepper. Set aside.

Using a serrated knife, split the bread in half. Layer the bresaola, mozzarella, arugula, basil, tomatoes, and caramelized onion over the bottom half of the bread. Drizzle with the dressing. Using a serrated knife, cut the bread into four equal pieces. Grill until the bread is golden and the cheese melts, 4 to 5 minutes per side, pressing each sandwich with a large spatula to flatten it as you grill it. Remove and serve.

GRILLED EGGPLANT, RED PEPPER, AND CHEESE SANDWICHES

THE MEDITERRANEAN boasts many a trinity of foods and flavors that go together in endless combination. Eggplant, red peppers, and cheese are among them, savored in infinite variety from one end of the region to the other.

MAKES 4 SERVINGS

1 medium round eggplant

Salt to taste

$\frac{1}{2}$ cup olive oil

1 garlic clove, minced

$\frac{1}{2}$ teaspoon crumbled dried thyme

Freshly ground black pepper to taste

2 red bell peppers

8 ($\frac{1}{2}$-inch) slices sourdough or other country-style fresh bread

3 ounces soft goat cheese

12 large fresh basil leaves

Wash and pat dry the eggplant. Slice into 8 or 12 equal rounds. Layer the eggplant slices in a sieve and season each layer with a little salt. Place a weight on top. Let stand for about 30 minutes. Remove, rinse, and pat dry.

Heat the grill to medium-low and set the rack about 4 inches from the heat source.

In a medium bowl, combine the olive oil, the garlic, thyme, and salt and pepper. Toss the eggplant and peppers in the mixture. Place first the peppers and then the eggplant on the grill and cook, turning once, until softened and lightly browned. The eggplant slices will take 7 to 8 minutes. The peppers will take about 12 minutes, and should char slightly on their skin side. Remove, place in a bowl, cover with plastic wrap, and let cool slightly. Peel, seed, and slice the peppers.

Place the bread on the grill to toast a little. Remove when warm and the grill marks are visible.

Spread a little goat cheese on each slice of bread. Use two or three slices each of the eggplant and peppers per sandwich. Place three basil leaves inside each. Serve immediately.

GRILLED PORTOBELLO AND ONION SANDWICHES

THESE SANDWICHES are a meal in themselves. The seasoning takes its cue from a northern Greek mushroom pie, flavored with paprika and mint.

MAKES 4 SERVINGS

2 medium red onions, halved

½ cup extra virgin olive oil

Salt and freshly ground black pepper to taste

4 very large portobello mushrooms caps, dark gills removed (save the stems for another use, such as for soup)

2 teaspoons chopped fresh mint

Smoked Hungarian sweet or hot paprika to taste

4 country-style bread rolls

4 ounces Greek Graviera cheese or Parmesan cheese, shaved

Heat the grill to medium-hot.

Toss the onions in a bowl with 2 tablespoons of the olive oil and a little salt and pepper.

Place on the grill rack and grill until the onions are very lightly charred, about 8 minutes. About halfway through grilling the onions, toss the mushrooms with 3 tablespoons more of the olive oil, salt, and pepper and grill until tender but meaty, 6 to 8 minutes. Remove the onions and mushrooms as they brown and slice thin. Toss with the mint and paprika and adjust the seasoning with additional salt and pepper.

Cut the bread rolls in half and brush the cut sides with the remaining 3 tablespoons olive oil. Grill until lightly browned and lined with grill marks. Remove. Place one-fourth of the mushroom-onion mixture on each bottom half of the bread. Add equal portions of shaved cheese. Cover the sandwiches with the top pieces of bread and serve immediately.

GRILLED CHICKEN PITA SANDWICHES WITH GOAT CHEESE

HERE'S ANOTHER MEX-MED hybrid that came out of the quick staff snacks that Juan serves to his kitchen crew at Pylos in New York City.

MAKES 4 SERVINGS

¼ cup extra virgin olive oil

1½ cups finely chopped red onions (about 1½ large)

3 garlic cloves, minced

1 to 2 teaspoons chili powder, or more to taste

3 cups shredded cooked chicken

1 cup fresh mint leaves, cut into thin ribbons

Salt and freshly ground black pepper to taste

2 cups mild, soft goat cheese or soft Greek feta, crumbled

4 large pita breads with pockets

2 tablespoons softened unsalted butter

Heat the grill to medium-hot.

You can sauté outdoors on the grill in a heavy cast-iron skillet or a non-stick skillet with a flameproof handle, or indoors in the kitchen. Heat the olive oil in the skillet and cook the onions, garlic, and chili powder together, stirring, until the onions are translucent, about 5 minutes. Add the chicken and toss to coat. Remove and toss in the mint. Season with salt and pepper. Mix in the cheese.

Fill each pita pocket with one-fourth of the chicken mixture. Rub or brush with the softened butter and grill for about 3 minutes per side, or until warmed through. Serve, cut into wedges if desired.

GRILLED GREEK CHEESE IN PITA

TOSS THIS QUICK snack on the grill for immediate gratification.

MAKES 4 SERVINGS

4 large pita breads with pockets

**1¹/₂ pounds Greek feta, cut into
¹/₄-inch slices**

**16 pickled pepperoncini
peppers, drained, seeded,
and coarsely chopped**

**16 large pitted Kalamata
olives, coarsely chopped**

**2 large, firm, ripe tomatoes,
cored and cut into
¹/₄-inch rounds**

**1 tablespoon finely
chopped fresh oregano
or marjoram leaves**

**Freshly ground black
pepper to taste**

**4 tablespoons extra
virgin olive oil**

Heat the grill to medium.

Carefully pull open the pita pockets without tearing the bread. Fill each pita pocket with equal amounts of feta, pepperoncini, chopped olives, and tomato slices. Sprinkle the filling with oregano and pepper. Press closed. Brush both sides with ¹/₂ tablespoon olive oil and grill, pressing lightly, until there are grill marks on the pita and the feta is almost melted. Remove and serve immediately.

mainly
PASTA

Pasta is a springboard for all sorts of grilled food because it provides the perfect, neutral, all-embracing backdrop to almost anything you can toss on the grill. It also provides a soft, textural foil to the crunch of many grilled foods and a bit of subtle, sating sweetness to the pleasantly charred flavor of many grilled foods. Pasta goes especially well with the whole range of summer vegetables, especially when it's too hot for richly sauced dishes with seafood.

All types of pasta can be mixed with grilled vegetables, seafood, and meats. I use shorter pasta, such as ziti, penne, and rigatoni, with vegetable dishes and spaghetti with seafood. The basic difference is that the short pasta and grilled vegetable dishes provide a closer marriage of flavors—different small chunks of different food you can pick up in one forkful. Larger pieces of seafood, such as langoustines, lobsters, even large shrimp, don't so much meld into pasta dishes as complement them.

PENNE WITH GRILLED EGGPLANT, TOMATOES, AND MOZZARELLA

THIS IS AN EASY, summery dish that cooks up in no time. It's also a time-tested roster of ingredients that is extremely versatile and has universal appeal.

MAKES 4 SERVINGS

1 (1-pound) eggplant, trimmed and cut into ½-inch-thick rounds

8 to 10 plum tomatoes, halved lengthwise

½ cup extra virgin olive oil, or more to toss with pasta

½ pound penne or rigatoni

8 ounces mozzarella, cut into ½-inch cubes

¼ cup chopped fresh flat-leaf parsley

⅓ cup shredded fresh basil leaves

2 tablespoons finely chopped fresh oregano leaves

1 large garlic clove, minced

Salt and freshly ground black pepper to taste

Heat the grill to medium.

Toss the eggplant slices and tomato halves with ¼ cup olive oil. Place the tomatoes on the grill cut side up over direct heat, and grill for 4 to 6 minutes, until the skins begin to char. Turn and continue grilling for another 1 to 2 minutes. Grill the eggplant slices over indirect heat for 6 to 7 minutes, turning, until tender and browned. Remove. Cut the tomatoes into 1-inch pieces. Cut the eggplant slices into quarters. Set aside, covered, to keep warm.

Bring a large pot of salted water to a rolling boil and boil the pasta until al dente, about 9 minutes. Remove and drain. Add the vegetables to the hot pasta together with the remaining ¼ cup olive oil, the mozzarella, herbs, garlic, and salt and pepper. Serve immediately.

SHORT PASTA TOSSED WITH GRILLED EGGPLANT-TOMATO SAUCE AND RICOTTA

THERE IS A SMALL pasta restaurant in Athens called Maltagliatti that we go to often. I borrowed this recipe from Yarek, the chef and owner. The dish is warm and comforting.

MAKES 4 SERVINGS

2 large eggplants, trimmed and cut lengthwise into $\frac{1}{4}$-inch-thick slices

$\frac{3}{4}$ cup extra virgin olive oil

Salt and freshly ground black pepper to taste

$\frac{1}{2}$ pound ziti, rigatoni, penne, or other short pasta

2 garlic cloves, finely chopped

3 large tomatoes, seeded and cut into $\frac{1}{2}$-inch cubes

$\frac{1}{4}$ cup finely chopped flat-leaf parsley

$1\frac{1}{2}$ cups whole-milk ricotta

Heat the grill to medium-hot.

In a large bowl, toss the eggplant slices with $\frac{1}{2}$ cup olive oil and salt and pepper. Place the eggplant slices on the grill and cook, turning once or twice, for about 8 minutes total or until soft and lined on both sides with grill marks. Remove, cool slightly, and cut into $\frac{1}{2}$-inch pieces.

Bring a large pot of salted water to a rolling boil (you can do this on the grill) and cook the pasta until al dente, about 9 minutes. Drain and toss with 2 tablespoons of the olive oil.

While the water is boiling for the pasta, heat the remaining 2 tablespoons olive oil in a large skillet (you can do this, too, on the grill, in a heavy skillet with a flameproof handle) and sauté the garlic for 1 minute. Add the tomatoes and cook over medium heat for 6 to 7 minutes. Add the eggplant pieces. Season with salt and pepper.

Transfer the pasta to a serving bowl and toss with the sauce, parsley, and ricotta. Adjust the seasoning with a little pepper and serve.

SPAGHETTI WITH GARLICKY GRILLED CLAM SAUCE

HERE'S A TAKE on a classic dish from New York City's Little Italy. Grilled shellfish acquire a subtle, smoky flavor quite different from their unctuous, sautéed counterparts.

MAKES 4 SERVINGS

1 pound spaghetti

40 large littleneck clams, soaked for 3 hours in cold water and scrubbed

½ cup extra virgin olive oil

4 garlic cloves, cut into thin slivers

¾ teaspoon red pepper flakes

½ cup dry white wine

⅓ cup sweet Muscat wine

Coarse sea salt and freshly ground black pepper to taste

½ cup finely chopped flat-leaf parsley

Strained fresh juice of 1 lemon

Heat the grill to medium-hot.

Bring a large pot of salted water to a rolling boil and cook the pasta for about 9 minutes, until al dente (you can do this on the grill). Drain the clams and discard their water.

While the pasta is cooking, grill the clams, in batches if necessary, until they open, 6 to 8 minutes. Set aside on a plate or platter as they open.

Drain the pasta, reserving 2 cups of the cooking liquid.

Heat the olive oil on the grill in a large, wide, heavy pot with flameproof handles and sauté the garlic and red pepper flakes for about 1 minute, just until the garlic softens. Add the wines and raise the heat to high. As soon as the alcohol cooks off, in 2 to 3 minutes, season with salt and pepper. (You can do this on your stovetop, too, but it's easier to keep all the ingredients concentrated around the grill.) Add the pasta and clams to the pot. Add enough of the pasta cooking liquid to dampen the spaghetti and keep it from sticking, then mix in the parsley and lemon juice and serve.

GREEK-STYLE PASTA WITH GRILLED LANGOUSTINES AND TOMATO SAUCE

PASTA WITH SEAFOOD, especially shrimp, lobster, and/or langoustines is a classic dish throughout Greece and Italy. On the Greek islands, where the catch is fresh, the dish is often served in tavernas by the sea, especially in the summer, as a crowd-pleaser and bestseller during the tourist season.

MAKES 4 SERVINGS

For the tomato sauce

1/3 cup extra virgin olive oil

2 garlic cloves, finely chopped

10 large, ripe tomatoes, peeled, seeded, and chopped or grated

3 fresh oregano sprigs

1 scant teaspoon sugar

Salt and freshly ground black pepper to taste

1/3 cup fish stock

3 tablespoons strained fresh lemon juice

1 garlic clove, finely chopped

1 tablespoon smooth Dijon mustard

2 tablespoons finely chopped flat-leaf parsley, plus additional for garnish

1/2 cup plus 2 tablespoons extra virgin olive oil

1 pound langoustines or large shrimp

1 pound spaghetti or linguine

Make the sauce: Heat the olive oil in a medium saucepan over medium heat and sauté the garlic, stirring, for 1 minute, or until soft. Do not burn. Add the tomatoes and oregano and cook, covered, until the tomatoes disintegrate and thicken, about 10 minutes. Add 1½ cups water, the sugar, salt, and pepper. Continue simmering with the lid ajar until the sauce is thick, about 15 minutes. Set aside, covered, to keep warm.

In a large bowl, whisk together the fish stock, lemon juice, garlic, mustard, and parsley. Slowly add the ½ cup olive oil and whisk until emulsified. If using langoustines, leave whole with shells; if using shrimp, peel and devein, but leave heads and tails on. Place the langoustines or shrimp in the marinade for 1 hour.

Heat the grill to medium-hot.

Bring a large pot of salted water to a rolling boil and cook the pasta until al dente, about 10 minutes. (You can do this on the grill.) Drain and toss with the 2 tablespoons olive oil.

Place the langoustines or shrimp on the grill and cook for 6 to 8 minutes, until the flesh is white as cotton and the heads are bright pink. Brush with the marinade as you grill. Remove and place under a foil tent to keep warm.

Serve the spaghetti on individual plates. Top with a little sauce, place a langoustine on each plate, and top with a little more salt. Sprinkle with fresh parsley and serve.

NOTE: You can remove the meat from the langoustines before serving, but the shells make for a more dramatic presentation.

GRILLED SHRIMP WITH ORZO, FETA, AND SMOKED TOMATOES

THIS IS A FAVORITE with my kids for whom seafood automatically means shrimp. The deep, sweet flavor of the tomatoes couples nicely with the tang imparted by the olives and balsamic.

MAKES 6 SERVINGS

2 pounds plum tomatoes

$\frac{1}{2}$ cup extra virgin olive oil

Salt and freshly ground black pepper to taste

1 to 2 teaspoons sugar

$\frac{1}{4}$ cup balsamic vinegar

1 small head garlic

1 pound orzo

2 pounds medium shrimp, peeled, deveined, tails removed

$\frac{1}{3}$ cup oil-cured black olives

$\frac{1}{4}$ pound Greek feta, cut into $\frac{1}{4}$-inch cubes

Strained fresh juice of 1 lemon

$\frac{1}{2}$ cup julienned fresh basil or $\frac{1}{3}$ cup chopped fresh oregano leaves

Lemon wedges and additional basil or oregano for garnish

Heat the grill to medium-hot.

Bring a large pot of lightly salted water to a boil.

Cut the tomatoes in half lengthwise, remove the stem ends, and gently squeeze out the seeds. Lightly oil a shallow, heavy metal baking pan large enough to hold the tomato halves in one layer. Toss the tomatoes with 3 tablespoons of the olive oil, the salt, pepper, and sugar and place cut side up in the pan. Sprinkle with the balsamic vinegar. Cover the pan with aluminum foil and place on the grill over indirect heat. Wrap the garlic head with double-strength aluminum foil and place on the grill rack over indirect heat, too. Close the lid on the grill (make sure the vents are open) and smoke the tomatoes and garlic for 20 to 25 minutes, until the tomatoes are soft and charred. Remove the tomatoes and set aside, covered, to keep warm. Keep the garlic on the grill.

Boil the orzo until al dente, about 12 minutes. Remove, drain, and toss with 3 to 4 tablespoons of olive oil.

While the orzo is boiling, toss the shrimp with salt and pepper and grill over the hottest part of the grill for 3 to 4 minutes per side. Remove. Remove the garlic from the grill, separate the cloves, and squeeze out the pulp into the orzo.

Toss the orzo with the tomatoes, shrimp, olives, any remaining olive oil, feta, lemon juice, and basil. Adjust the seasoning with additional salt and pepper. Garnish with fresh lemon wedges and fresh basil or oregano. Serve warm.

WHOLE WHEAT PASTA WITH GRILLED VEGETABLES CRUMBLED FETA

A GREEK-INSPIRED version of pasta primavera.

MAKES 6 SERVINGS

10 plum tomatoes, halved

2 large red onions

3 medium zucchini

1 head garlic

1 pound whole wheat penne

6 tablespoons extra virgin olive oil, or more as desired

Salt and freshly ground black pepper to taste

^{2}/$_3$ cup pitted Kalamata olives, coarsely chopped

^{1}/$_2$ pound Greek feta, coarsely cumbled

^{1}/$_2$ cup shredded fresh basil leaves

2 to 3 tablespoons balsamic vinegar

Heat the grill to medium-hot.

Cut the tomatoes in half lengthwise. Cut the onions into quarters. Trim the zucchini and cut into ^{1}/$_4$-inch strips. Wrap the garlic in aluminum foil.

Bring a large pot of salted water to a rolling boil and boil the pasta until al dente, about 12 minutes. Drain, toss with 3 tablespoons of the olive oil, and set aside.

Toss the tomatoes, zucchini, and onions with the remaining 3 tablespoons olive oil, salt, and pepper. Oil the grill rack. Place the tomatoes cut side up and the onion quarters on the grill rack over direct heat. Place the wrapped garlic over indirect heat in one corner of the grill. Grill the tomatoes for 2 to 4 minutes, until the skins begin to char; turn and grill for another 2 minutes. Grill the onions for 4 to 5 minutes, until they also char. Place the zucchini strips on the grill for about a minute on each side.

Remove the vegetables from the grill. Coarsely chop the tomatoes and add them, with their juices, to the pasta. Coarsely chop the onions and cut the zucchini into ^{1}/$_2$-inch pieces. Add to the pasta. Add the olives, feta, and basil. Open the garlic and squeeze out the pulp. Add it to the pasta. Add the balsamic vinegar and additional olive oil to taste. Adjust the seasoning with salt and pepper, toss, and serve.

PASTA AND BEAN SALAD WITH GRILLED CELERY, TOMATOES, AND OLIVES

THIS RECIPE HARKENS back to Greek Jewish recipes from the Ionian period for a kind of soup/stew made with pasta, mottled beans, and celery. It's a hearty combination I have developed into something suitable for the grill.

MAKES 6 SERVINGS

$\frac{1}{3}$ **pound borlotti or mottled beans, soaked according to package directions, or 1 (15$\frac{1}{2}$-ounce) can, drained**

1 bay leaf, as needed

3 celery stalks, trimmed

10 large plum tomatoes, halved lengthwise

4 to 6 tablespoons extra virgin olive oil

Salt and freshly ground black pepper to taste

$\frac{1}{2}$ **pound small elbow macaroni**

$\frac{1}{2}$ **cup Kalamata olives, pitted, rinsed, drained, and coarsely chopped**

1 medium red onion, finely chopped

1 garlic clove, minced

$\frac{1}{2}$ **cup chopped fresh basil leaves**

$\frac{1}{2}$ **teaspoon dried thyme**

$\frac{1}{2}$ **cup chopped flat-leaf parsley**

2 to 4 tablespoons balsamic vinegar

Placed the soaked beans in a large pot of cold water and bring to a boil. Add the bay leaf. Reduce the heat and simmer the beans, uncovered, for about 1 hour, or until tender without disintegrating. Remove from the heat, drain, and rinse in a colander under cold water. Remove the bay leaf. Set aside. If using canned beans, drain and rinse with cold water in a colander.

Heat the grill to medium-hot.

Cut the celery stalks in half lengthwise. Place in a bowl with the tomato halves and toss with 2 tablespoons of the olive oil, salt, and pepper. Grill the celery over the hottest part of the grill, turning until lightly charred on both sides, about 10 minutes. Grill the tomatoes over medium-high heat, cut side up, until the skins begin to char, 2 to 4 minutes, then turn to grill on the cut side, another 1 to 2 minutes. Remove. Cool slightly and chop, reserving their juices. Cut the celery into $\frac{1}{2}$-inch pieces.

Boil the pasta in salted water until al dente, about 2 minutes. Drain and toss with 2 tablespoons of the olive oil. Add the beans, olives, celery, and tomatoes to the pasta. Add the chopped onion, garlic, and herbs. Season with 2 tablespoons vinegar and salt and pepper. Adjust the seasoning with additional vinegar, olive oil, salt, and pepper.

KEBABS

Does any food capture the image of Mediterranean grilling better than a glistening kebab? For years, one of my favorite childhood foods on our Sunday outings to various Greek family restaurants were the gargantuan souvlakia threaded with cubes of lamb, tomatoes, onions, and peppers and swaddled in warm, grilled pita bread. The dish is still irresistible to me, especially the soft, charred tomatoes and the sweet, slightly burnt onions.

The notion of threading food onto a stick and cooking it over embers is indeed very old, predating cookware itself. It doesn't take a great leap of imagination to realize all the primordial chords that grilled, skewered meats touch upon, helping us recall mythical feasts and ancient memories that are part of the tapestry of human existence. The skewer might once have been an ingenious, spontaneous tool of necessity, but today it is a gourmet's play thing. Kebabs are fun.

In the Mediterranean, all sorts of dishes are threaded onto all sorts of skewers small and large, wooden or metal, even on sticks like sugarcane and rosemary stalks. They go by different names: kebabs or kabobs in the Eastern Mediterranean; souvla or souvlaki in Greece; pinchitos in Spain; and brochettes in France.

There is an immediacy to all of these dishes that diners find especially appealing, and it's no wonder that skewered foods are such a hit in restaurants the world over. In Greece, for example, there are whole restaurants devoted just to grilled, skewered foods, mainly meats. They are called *souvlatzidika* and they often serve heroic-size portions of grilled cubes of meat on a stick with a whole battery of other accompaniments, such as fries, tzatziki, tomato salad, and grilled eggplant spread.

Kebabs needle the imagination. As long as it tastes good, you can thread almost anything onto a stick and grill it. The Spanish probably have first place in the imagination arena, and skewered foods—not necessarily grilled, though—are among the country's favorite tapas.

BREADED MOZZARELLA AND CHERRY
TOMATO BROCHETTES

THESE TOMATO-CHEESE kebabs are perfect outdoor party food as long as someone mans the grill and serves these up immediately, before the cheese gets cold. You can substitute other mild-flavored cheese for the mozzarella, such as a firm Greek kefalograviera or Italian scamorza.

MAKES 8 APPETIZER SERVINGS

8 (6-inch) wooden skewers

1 cup plain bread crumbs

Salt and freshly ground black pepper to taste

2 scant teaspoons garlic powder

2 tablespoons fresh basil leaves

2 to 3 tablespoons extra virgin olive oil

16 cherry tomatoes

16 miniature mozzarella balls or 24 ounces mozzarella (1½ blocks), cut into 16 cubes

1 egg, lightly beaten

Vegetable oil for brushing grill rack

Soak the skewers in water for 30 minutes.

Heat the grill to medium-hot and set the grill rack about 4 inches from the heat source.

Combine the bread crumbs, salt, pepper, half the garlic powder, and 1 tablespoon basil in a shallow bowl and set aside. Place the olive oil, remaining garlic powder, salt, pepper, and remaining basil in a separate small bowl and toss the tomatoes in the mixture.

Drain the mozzarella and pat dry. Have the beaten egg in another, separate shallow bowl. Toss the mozzarella balls in the egg, toss in the bread crumbs, then dip in the egg again.

Thread each of the skewers with two pieces of mozzarella and two tomatoes, alternating between each. Wipe the grill rack with oil. Place the skewers on the grill and grill, turning, for about 3 minutes total, until the cheese is crisp on the outside and beginning to melt and the tomatoes are lightly charred. Remove and serve immediately.

CLASSIC GREEK CHICKEN KEBABS

CHICKEN SOUVLAKI is classic fare in every corner of the eastern Mediterranean. The Greek flavors in this version come from the trio of lemon, garlic, and oregano.

MAKES 8 SERVINGS

1¹/₂ pounds boneless, skinless chicken breast halves, cut into 32 (1-inch) pieces

4 tablespoons extra virgin olive oil

2 tablespoons fresh lemon juice

4 large garlic cloves, minced

2 teaspoons dried mint, preferably Greek

2 teaspoons dried Greek oregano

1 teaspoon salt

1 teaspoon freshly ground black pepper

8 (12-inch) metal skewers

32 fresh bay leaves, soaked in water for 30 minutes, or 32 large mint leaves

8 red onions, quartered

Toss the chicken with the olive oil, lemon juice, minced garlic, dried mint, oregano, salt, and pepper. Let stand, covered and refrigerated, for 1 hour.

Heat the grill to very hot.

Alternating between each, thread each skewer with four chicken chunks, four fresh bay or mint leaves, and four onion pieces.

Grill the kebabs over high, direct heat for about 15 minutes, turning to brown on all sides. Baste with the leftover marinade while grilling, carefully, as the oil will flare up. Serve hot.

CHICKEN KEBABS MARINATED IN CUMIN YOGURT

YOGURT IS a popular addition to marinades in Greece and Turkey. The spices in this dish make a nice, pungent foil to the cooling qualities of the yogurt.

MAKES 6 SERVINGS

1 cup Greek-style strained yogurt

⅓ cup extra virgin olive oil

1 tablespoon Dijon mustard

1 heaping tablespoon ground cumin

Fresh juice of 1 large lemon

3 garlic cloves, minced

Salt and freshly ground black pepper to taste

3 boneless, skinless chicken breasts, cut into 1-inch cubes

Vegetable oil for brushing grill rack

2 large red onions, peeled, quartered lengthwise, then halved

24 cherry tomatoes, stems removed

2 green bell peppers, cored, seeded, and cut into 1-inch squares

6 (15-inch) metal skewers

Lemon wedges for garnish

Combine the yogurt, olive oil, mustard, cumin, lemon juice, garlic, salt, and pepper in a bowl. Toss in the chicken cubes and marinate, covered and refrigerated, for 2 hours.

Heat the grill to medium-hot and lightly oil the grill rack.

Thread the chicken, onion pieces, tomatoes, and bell peppers onto skewers, alternating vegetables. Grill over medium heat, turning, until the chicken is cooked through and golden on all sides, 20 to 25 minutes. Serve hot with lemon wedges on the side.

CLASSIC SHISH KEBAB

ANYONE WHO has traveled to Greece or Turkey, or parts of the Middle East, has most likely sat down to a meal of tangy shish kebab. The combination of grilled lamb, peppers, onions, tomatoes, and herbs is irresistible. I've no wonder immigrants exported this dish to Greek and Turkish restaurants far from the Eastern Mediterranean.

MAKES 4 SERVINGS

For the marinade

2 tablespoons coarse salt

Freshly ground black pepper to taste

2 tablespoons dried Greek oregano

2 tablespoons minced garlic

½ cup extra virgin olive oil

⅓ cup strained fresh lemon juice

1½ pounds boneless lamb leg or shoulder, cut into 1-inch cubes

2 green bell peppers, cored, seeded, and cut into eighths

2 red onions, peeled and cut into eighths

16 cherry tomatoes, stems removed, or 4 large ripe tomatoes, cored and cut into quarters

16 whole fresh bay leaves, soaked in water for 30 minutes

4 (10-inch) flat metal skewers

4 pita breads

8 teaspoons extra virgin olive oil

Make the marinade: Combine the ingredients in a bowl and toss in the lamb cubes. Cover and refrigerate for at least 1 hour and up to 3 hours.

Heat the grill to hot.

Thread the meat, peppers, onions, tomatoes, and bay leaves onto the skewers, alternating ingredients. Brush the skewers with the marinade. Grill the kebabs, turning on all sides, until done. For rare meat, figure on 8 to 10 minutes total grilling time; for medium, 12 to 14 minutes; and for well-done, about 20 minutes. Times will vary slightly according to individual units. While grilling, brush every few minutes with the marinade—carefully, as it will flair up.

While the skewers are cooking, brush the pita breads with half the olive oil and grill slightly. Turn, brush the other side with the remaining oil, and grill lightly. The bread should not toast, but rather should be soft and pliant.

Serve the shish kebabs on the skewers atop the pita breads.

TURKISH-STYLE LAMB KEBABS

WHEN WE had our restaurant on Ikarea, Yiorgia, one of our waitresses had just come back from a trip to Turkey. One night after all the customers had gone home, she stood at the grill and made these kebabs for our dinner.

MAKES 4 SERVINGS

For the dry rub

2 teaspoons cumin seeds, coarsely ground

1 teaspoon coriander seeds, coarsely ground

1/2 teaspoon sumac (optional)

1/2 teaspoon ground cinnamon

1 teaspoon dried thyme

1 scant teaspoon salt

1/2 teaspoon cracked black peppercorns

1/2 cup extra virgin olive oil, or more as needed

2 pounds boneless leg of lamb, trimmed and cut into 20 (1-inch) cubes

4 (10-inch) metal skewers

4 tablespoons strained fresh lemon juice

1 red onion

1/2 teaspoon sweet paprika

Dash of cayenne pepper

3 tablespoons finely chopped flat-leaf parsley

4 pita breads

1 1/2 cups Greek- or Mediterranean-style strained yogurt

Make the dry rub: Combine the ingredients in a medium bowl. Place 4 tablespoons of the olive oil in a medium bowl and toss the meat to coat in the oil. Place the meat in the bowl with the spice mixture and toss to coat all over. Let stand for 15 to 30 minutes.

Heat the grill to medium-hot.

Thread five pieces of meat onto each skewer. Whisk together the remaining 4 tablespoons olive oil and 3 tablespoons of the lemon juice. Place the meat skewers on the grill and grill, turning several times, for 10 to 15 minutes, or to desired doneness. Brush with the olive oil–lemon mixture as the skewers grill.

In the meantime, peel and halve the onion. Using a mandolin or very sharp knife, cut the onion into paper-thin slices. Toss by hand in a bowl with the paprika, cayenne, and remaining tablespoon of lemon juice. Add the parsley and combine.

Grill the pita breads lightly, brushing, if desired, with extra olive oil.

To serve, place the skewers on individual plates or a platter, scatter with the raw onion mixture, and place a dollop of yogurt on the side. Serve the pitas on the same plates or on the side.

LAMB, QUINCE, AND ONION SKEWERS

MY FRIEND Nena Ismirnoglou, one of the top women chefs in Athens, opened a vast meze restaurant in the heart of the city. She set out to reinvent the meze, with a host of new dishes that gave a nod to tradition but offered something fresh. The combination of lamb and quince is traditional, but it's usually in the form of a rich, wintry stew. Nena disentangled the classic Greek dish and came up with this beautiful grilled souvlaki. If you can't find quince, use firm apples.

MAKES 4 SERVINGS

For the marinade

1 cup dry red wine

1/3 cup balsamic vinegar

1 teaspoon dried Greek mint

1/2 teaspoon cracked black peppercorns

Salt to taste

1/2 cup extra virgin Greek olive oil

2 garlic cloves, crushed

1 cinnamon stick

1 large bay leaf, cracked

3 whole cloves

4 allspice berries

2 medium quince, peeled

1 lemon, halved

2 large red onions

1 1/2 pounds boneless leg of lamb, trimmed and cut into 16 (2-inch) cubes

4 (8-inch) metal skewers

Vegetable oil for brushing grill rack

2 tablespoons olive oil

Make the marinade: In a medium bowl, whisk together the red wine, vinegar, mint, peppercorns, and salt. Slowly drizzle in the olive oil and whisk until emulsified. Stir in the garlic, cinnamon, bay leaf, cloves, and allspice.

Using a large, heavy chef's knife, cut each quince into four wedges. Rub with the cut lemon to keep from discoloring. Carefully remove the core and pits in each wedge, then cut in half again to get a total of eight pieces per quince. Peel and cut the onions in quarters lengthwise, and cut each quarter in half to get a total of eight smaller pieces of onion.

Toss the lamb, quince, and onions in the marinade and let marinate for 4 to 8 hours.

Heat the grill to medium-hot.

Remove the lamb, quince, and onions from the marinade and set aside the liquid. Thread the lamb, quince, and onion pieces onto the skewers, alternating the ingredients.

Lightly oil the grill rack and brush each skewer with a little olive oil. Place on the rack and grill, turning, until the lamb is medium-rare and the quince has softened, 3 to 4 minutes per side. Brush each skewer with the marinade as you grill the kebabs. Remove and serve immediately.

PROVENÇAL-STYLE LAMB BROCHETTES

AS A Greek cook, it's always interesting to me to see certain ingredients that I associate so closely with my own traditions—in this case lamb and organ meats—prepared slightly differently. Lamb souvlaki is a common dish in Greece; so are kidneys and livers; and common, too, is the technique of grating onions. But the specific combination below, decidedly not Greek, is yet another reminder to me how similar, yet unique are all the cuisines of the Mediterranean.

MAKES 6 SERVINGS

12 lamb kidneys or 2 young lambs' livers (optional)

1/3 cup extra virgin olive oil

Salt and freshly ground black pepper to taste

2 tablespoons dried thyme

1 large onion, grated

1 1/2 pounds boneless lamb loin, cut into 1-inch cubes

Vegetable oil for brushing grill rack

6 (8-inch) metal skewers

Lemon wedges for garnish

Remove the gristle from the kidneys and wash well, or if using livers, wash well.

Combine the olive oil, salt and pepper, thyme, and grated onion with its juices in a bowl, and toss the lamb and kidneys or liver in the mixture. Marinate, covered, for at least 3 hours or overnight.

Heat the grill to hot and oil the grill rack.

Thread the meat cubes onto skewers. Place on the grill and cook for about 15 minutes, turning, for medium-rare lamb, or longer, to desired doneness. Serve immediately, with lemon wedges on the side.

PROVENÇAL-STYLE BEEF TENDERLOINS WITH GARLIC, BACON, AND ANCHOVIES

I STUMBLED on this dish years ago in a small restaurant outside of Aix. We had shipped our car from Port Elizabeth, New Jersey, to Antwerp and were making our way south and east, en route to Greece. We wended our way through Provence leisurely, savoring every meal and every glass of wine.

MAKES 4 SERVINGS

For the sauce

3 anchovy fillets

1 cup extra virgin olive oil

1 garlic clove, finely chopped

Freshly ground black pepper to taste

2 garlic cloves, finely chopped

1½ pounds boneless beef tenderloin, cut into 8 equal rounds

Salt to taste

½ teaspoon ground white pepper

2 teaspoons dried rosemary

4 slices fatback or Canadian bacon

4 (12-inch) metal skewers

Make the sauce: Cut the anchovies into small pieces. Place in the bowl of a food processor with 2 tablespoons of the olive oil, the garlic, and pepper and pulse on and off until puréed. Place in a jar with the remaining olive oil. Set aside for at least 6 hours or up to 1 week, sealed and refrigerated.

Squeeze a little pinch of garlic onto each of the beef rounds. Combine the salt, white pepper, and rosemary and rub over the meat.

Heat the grill to medium-hot.

Cut each bacon slice into three equal pieces. Thread a piece of bacon, one beef round, another piece of bacon, one more beef round, and one last piece of bacon onto each of the skewers. Place the skewers on the grill and baste with the olive oil–anchovy sauce. Grill for about 4 minutes on each side, or until the meat is seared on the outside but tender and rare within. Remove and serve immediately.

SPANISH-STYLE KEBABS WITH SMOKED SAUSAGE AND SHRIMP

THE ROBUST combination of seafood and sausage speaks tomes about the vibrant foods of Spain.

MAKES 4 SERVINGS

Vegetable oil for
brushing grill rack

10 ounces smoked sausage
or chorizo, cut into
16 (1-inch) rounds

16 large shrimp, peeled,
deveined, heads removed
but tails intact

2 red bell peppers,
cored, seeded, and cut into
8 (1-inch) squares each

4 tablespoons extra
virgin olive oil

Salt and freshly ground
black pepper to taste

4 (10-inch) metal skewers

Fresh juice of
1 large lemon

Heat the grill to hot. Oil the grill rack.

Toss the sausage, shrimp, and peppers with the olive oil, salt, and pepper. Alternating among the sausage rounds, shrimp, and pepper squares, thread four pieces of each onto each skewer. Grill for 8 to 9 minutes, turning. Remove, sprinkle with fresh lemon juice, and serve.

PINCHITOS—SPANISH PORK KEBABS

PINCHITOS—SMALL KEBABS—are made in every conceivable combination all over Spain, as one of the country's countless tapa items. The cumin, saffron, and cayenne in this recipe pay homage to the aromas not only of Spain but also of North Africa.

MAKES 4 TO 6 SERVINGS

1 pound boneless pork loin, cut into 1-inch cubes

2 lemons

1 orange

3 tablespoons ground cumin

⅓ cup extra virgin olive oil

3 garlic cloves, minced

1 scant teaspoon cayenne pepper, or less to taste

½ teaspoon saffron threads

Salt and freshly ground black pepper to taste

Vegetable oil for brushing grill rack

6 (10-inch) metal skewers

Rinse and drain the pork. Wipe dry with paper towels.

Cut the lemons and orange in half and squeeze their juices into a bowl large enough to hold the pork cubes. Mix in the cumin, olive oil, garlic, cayenne, saffron, salt, and pepper. Toss the pork in the marinade. Add the cut lemons and orange to the marinade, cover, and refrigerate for 4 to 24 hours.

Heat the grill to medium hot and oil the grill rack. Thread the pork cubes onto skewers. Grill, turning and basting with the marinade, for about 15 minutes or until the pork is cooked through and nicely browned. Serve hot.

ground
MEAT
from med heaven

Sunday lunch is the time we visit restaurants as a family, usually preferring traditional places with home-cooked food and a good grill. The kids go for the grilled stuff, and among their favorites is the Greek answer to an all-American burger. We call it *bifteki* in the language of Homer.

Grilled ground meats come in several classic shapes all along the Mediterranean coast. Grilled meatballs and biftekia are common fare, but so are the more eastern renditions on grilled ground meat, shaped along a stick and eaten as street food from Ankara to Damascus.

Grilled meats sparkle with the countless seasonings that make Mediterranean food so flavorful, from earthy herbs like oregano and basil, to sweet-and-sour marinades of honey, vinegar, and spices, to robust garlic. A good bottle of wine, good company, and a few grilled side dishes are all you need to make these grilled meat main courses complete.

As a nod to American backyard gourmets, I include several Mediterranean-inspired hamburgers. Burgers have been co-opted and adopted so that almost every Mediterranean country has its own version, some with ground lamb, others with ground beef, garnished with the whole gamut of national cheeses, from feta to mozzarella to Cabrales.

GRILLED BEEF BURGERS WITH RED PEPPERS AND ROQUEFORT

A WINEMAKER FRIEND described the flavor of this dish in wine terms and I borrow his words: "There is energy on the palate with the first bite. The sweet roasted red peppers play against the luxurious acidity of the Roquefort and together balance this simple Mediterranean burger."

MAKES 8 SERVINGS

1½ pounds ground beef chuck

1 pound ground sirloin

1 medium red onion, puréed in a food processor or grated, with juices

2 tablespoons tomato paste, preferably sun-dried

3 tablespoons balsamic vinegar

2 tablespoons dry red wine

2 teaspoons ground rosemary

Salt and freshly ground black pepper to taste

Vegetable oil for brushing grill rack

4 large red bell peppers

2 tablespoons extra virgin olive oil, plus extra for shaping burgers

⅓ pound Roquefort or other good-quality blue cheese

8 (4 × 4-inch) squares plain or rosemary-scented focaccia, cut in half and opened

In a large bowl, combine the ground chuck and sirloin, the onion and its juices, the tomato paste, 2 tablespoons balsamic vinegar, the red wine, rosemary, and salt and pepper. Knead until well blended. Cover and refrigerate for 1 hour.

Heat the grill to medium-hot and lightly oil the grill rack.

Place the peppers on the grill and cook, turning, until blistered and soft, about 15 minutes. Remove with tongs and transfer to a bowl. Cover the bowl with plastic wrap and set aside until the peppers are cool enough to handle. Peel and seed the peppers. Strain and set aside their juices. Cut the peppers into thin strips, about ⅛ inch thick. Combine with the olive oil, remaining tablespoon balsamic and the crumbled Roquefort and set aside.

Wipe the grill clean with an oiled cloth. Rub the palms of your hands with a little oil (it helps keep the burgers from sticking on the grill). Shape the meat into eight large burgers. Grill the burgers for about 5 minutes per side for medium, 6 to 7 minutes per side for well done. Remove and set aside covered to keep warm.

Place the focaccia on the grill cut side down and grill for about 1 minute, to crisp slightly and to line lightly with grill marks. Remove. Serve the burgers on the focaccia, and top each with a tablespoon or so of the red pepper-Roquefort relish.

GREEK LAMB BIFTEKIA STUFFED WITH SPICED FETA

GRILLED LAMB patties are classic Greek taverna fare, the kind of thing you order for the kids on a typical Sunday family outing.

MAKES 8 SERVINGS

2½ pounds ground lamb

4 large garlic cloves, pressed

4 tablespoons dried mint or
½ cup finely chopped fresh mint

4 tablespoons finely chopped
fresh oregano leaves

Salt and freshly ground
black pepper to taste

4 to 6 tablespoons extra
virgin olive oil

Vegetable oil for
brushing grill rack

½ pound Greek feta

1 scant teaspoon
cayenne pepper

1 tablespoon plus
1 teaspoon fresh lemon juice

4 ripe but firm large fresh
tomatoes, preferably beefsteaks

8 pita breads

Combine the lamb, garlic, mint, oregano, salt, and pepper in a large bowl and knead. Add 2 to 4 tablespoons of the olive oil as needed while working with the meat. The mixture should be dense but slightly unctuous. Cover with plastic wrap and refrigerate for 1 hour.

Heat the grill to medium-hot and lightly oil the grill rack.

Combine the feta, cayenne, and lemon juice in a small bowl, mashing with a fork to form a thick paste. Divide the feta mixture into eight equal portions, about a heaping tablespoon each, and shape into a small ball.

Core and cut the tomatoes into ½-inch cubes and place in a bowl together with their juices. Season lightly with salt.

Divide the seasoned lamb into eight equal portions. Rub the palms of your hands with a little oil (it helps keep the burgers from sticking on the grill). Form the burgers and using your thumb, make an indention in the center of each burger. Fill the indentation with the feta mixture and patch the meat over the top with your fingers to seal the feta within the burger.

Place the burgers on the grill and cook for 4 to 5 minutes per side for medium. Remove and set aside covered to keep warm. Brush the pita breads with the remaining olive oil and grill for a minute on each side, to warm and soften. Remove. Place the pitas on a platter or on individual serving plates and place a lamb burger on top of each. Spoon the tomatoes over the mixture and serve.

TURKISH LAMB BURGERS WITH ONION JUICE MARINADE

THIS CLASSIC Turkish marinade is a startling addition to the burgers, unlike what most Americans are used to adding to a classic burger. The spices add a decidedly Eastern component and the onion marinade enhances it.

MAKES 8 SERVINGS

For the onion juice marinade

2 large white onions

3 tablespoons extra virgin olive oil

1/2 teaspoon salt

1 pound fatty ground chuck

1/2 pound ground lamb

1 large yellow onion, grated or puréed in a food processor

2 teaspoons ground cumin

2 teaspoons sweet paprika

1/2 teaspoon cayenne pepper

1/2 cup finely chopped flat-leaf parsley

2 tablespoons extra virgin olive oil, plus extra for shaping burgers

Salt and freshly ground black pepper to taste

Vegetable oil for brushing grill rack

8 pita breads, cut in half crosswise

Make the marinade: Peel and wash the onions, then grate along the fine-holed side of a manual cheese grater. (Alternatively, pulverize the onions in a food processor.) Place the onions in a fine-mesh strainer or in cheesecloth and press or squeeze to extract the juices. You should have about 1 cup of juice. Discard the pulp. Mix the onion juice with the olive oil and salt. Set aside.

In a large bowl, combine the ground chuck and lamb, grated yellow onion, cumin, paprika, cayenne, parsley, olive oil and salt and pepper and knead well. Cover with plastic wrap and refrigerate for 1 hour.

Heat the grill to hot and lightly oil the grill rack.

Rub the palms of your hands with a little oil (it helps keep the burgers from sticking on the grill). Shape the ground meat mixture into eight burgers. Place on the grill and cook, turning and brushing with the onion juice marinade, for 4 to 5 minutes per side for medium, 6 to 7 minutes per side for well-done. Remove and set aside, covered, to keep warm.

Lightly grill the pita halves. Serve the burgers with the pitas on a platter or on individual plates, and spoon the remaining onion juice marinade over the cooked burgers for additional flavor.

TURKISH-STYLE GRILLED MEAT PATTIES

ALL OVER the Mediterranean lamb is a blank slate for all kinds of spices and herbs. This recipe is less spicy than the lamb burgers from Turkey on page 105. The cinnamon adds a sweet, aromatic note.

MAKES 4 SERVINGS

1 pound boneless leg of lamb, finely ground

2 medium onions, grated and juices reserved

½ cup finely chopped flat-leaf parsely

1 teaspoon dried thyme

½ teaspoon ground cinnamon

½ teaspoon cayenne pepper

Salt and freshly ground black pepper to taste

Onion Juice Marinade (page 105)

4 pita breads

Greek-style strained yogurt

Heat the grill to medium-hot.

In a large bowl combine the lamb, onions, parsley, thyme, cinnamon, cayenne, salt, and pepper. Knead the mixture for 6 to 7 minutes. Divide the mixture into eight equal portions and shape into rounded ovals.

Place the meat ovals on the grill. Grill, turning and basting with the onion-juice marinade, for about 5 minutes, or until browned and cooked through. Serve with grilled pita bread and a side of cool, thick Greek yogurt.

SPICY TOMATO-RUBBED LAMB PATTIES WITH PINE NUTS

THESE SIMPLE patties speak the spice language of the eastern Aegean, where aromatic seasonings such as cinnamon and allspice are often paired with meat and tomatoes. The addition of pine nuts lends these patties a decidedly Turkish and Middle Eastern accent.

MAKES 4 TO 6 SERVINGS

For the spicy tomato rub

3 large garlic cloves

1/2 teaspoon salt

1/4 cup extra virgin olive oil

1 tablespoon tomato paste

1/2 teaspoon cayenne pepper or red pepper flakes

Freshly ground black pepper to taste

1/2 teaspoon ground allspice

1/2 teaspoon ground cinnamon

1/2 teaspoon ground cumin

1 scant teaspoon dried thyme

1/4 to 1/2 cup water

1 tablespoon unsalted butter

1/4 cup pine nuts

1 pound boneless leg of lamb, ground twice

2 red onions, grated

1/2 cup chopped fresh flat-leaf parsley

2 teaspoons crumbled dried mint

Salt and freshly ground black pepper to taste

Oil for shaping the burgers

Make the spicy rub: Using a mortar and pestle, crush the garlic together with the salt. Slowly add the remaining ingredients for the rub, working them in until a smooth loose paste is formed. (You may also do this in a food processor.) Set aside.

Heat the grill to medium-hot.

Melt the butter in a nonstick skillet over medium heat. When it bubbles, add the pine nuts and toss with a wooden spoon until lightly browned, about 4 minutes. Remove and set aside.

Combine the lamb, onions, parsley, mint, and salt and pepper in a large bowl and knead for 6 to 7 minutes. Lightly oil the palms of your hands to facilitate shaping the burgers. Divide the mixture into four or six equal portions and shape each into a patty. Make an indentation in each patty and stuff with a scant tablespoon of pine nuts. Pinch close and smooth over to seal the meat over the nuts.

Place the patties on the grill and brush the tops with the tomato rub. Flip when the bottom is browned and brush the surface with more of the tomato mixture. Grill for a total of 5 to 6 minutes for a rare burger, about 8 minutes for medium.

Serve immediately, with a green salad, if desired.

JUICY SUN-DRIED TOMATO BURGERS

THIS RECIPE came about after I experimented with a sun-dried tomato and caper tapenade that a friend, the owner of Gaea Foods, produces in Greece. You can find the product in high-end supermarkets throughout the United States or substitute chopped sun-dried tomatoes packed in olive oil.

MAKES 6 SERVINGS

1 cup chopped sun-dried tomatoes in olive oil

½ medium red onion

1 pound ground chuck or sirloin

1 pound ground pork

2 tablespoons dried basil

2 teaspoons dried Greek oregano

Salt and freshly ground black pepper to taste

Vegetable oil for brushing grill rack

6 (¼-inch) slices fresh mozzarella

6 hamburger buns

1 large red onion, sliced into thin rings

18 arugula or large basil leaves, trimmed

Drain the tomatoes and set aside their oil. Pulverize the chopped tomatoes at high speed in a food processor. Remove and set aside. Repeat with the onion, processing until almost liquid.

Combine the ground beef and pork, puréed tomatoes, puréed onion and its juices, 3 tablespoons of the tomato oil, the basil, oregano, and salt and pepper and knead well so that all the ingredients are evenly combined. Shape the burgers into six equal patties. Cover and refrigerate for 30 minutes.

Heat the grill to medium-hot and lightly oil the grill rack.

Grill the burgers about 5 minutes per side for medium. Add one slice of mozzarella to the top of each burger, and as soon as it begins to melt, remove the burger.

Lightly grill the buns. Serve the burgers on the buns and top with a few thin slices of onion and the arugula or basil leaves.

TURKISH-STYLE LAMB KEBABS

GROUND LAMB kebabs, pressed like lollipops along metal and wooden skewers, are one of the great dishes of Turkish cuisine.

MAKES 10 SERVINGS

2 pounds finely ground lamb

1½ cups very finely chopped or grated onions, drained in a colander

3 large garlic cloves, finely minced

1 cup chopped flat-leaf parsley

½ teaspoon cayenne pepper, or more to taste

Salt and freshly ground black pepper to taste

½ to 1 cup plain, fresh fine bread crumbs

10 (15-inch) metal skewers

2 medium red onions, sliced paper-thin

1 scant teaspoon sumac

Vegetable oil for brushing grill rack

⅓ cup unsalted butter, melted

10 pita breads

In a large bowl, combine the ground meat, onions, garlic, parsley, cayenne, and salt and pepper and knead well for 7 or 8 minutes to combine thoroughly. Add enough of the bread crumbs, kneading, until the mixture is dense and sticky.

Heat the grill to medium.

Have a bowl of water set nearby to dampen the palms of your hands. With wet hands, take about one-eighth (¼ pound) of the mixture and shape it around a skewer. Dampen your hands continuously and shape the meat into a cylinder by squeezing it along the skewer and against it, and smooth it out, again with dampened hands. The final "sausage" should be about 8 inches long. Continue with remaining meat and skewers.

Combine the onions and sumac and set aside.

Lightly oil the grill rack. Place the kebabs on the grill and grill for 3 to 4 minutes on each side, brushing with a little melted butter.

Grill the pita breads lightly, turning once and brushing each side with butter.

Place the kebabs over the warm pita and garnish with the sliced onion relish.

searious
MEAT

In Castile you go to the asadores, in Larissa (Greece) to the psistaries, and in France to the grillades—all in the name of seeking out what few Mediterranean home cooks do with ease: grill large cuts of meat to lavish perfection, oozing tangy juices the color of the wine-dark sea. These are the grill houses, usually—but not always—large, friendly, family restaurants where kids, parents, grandparents, and a few adjunct relatives or friends exercise their Mediterranean right to a long, leisurely meal every Sunday. That's not to say they don't fill up midweek, too. Athens, where I live, is experiencing a grilled meat craze, with restaurants named Meat-ing, Meat-me, and Meat Square popping up all over the city to immediate success.

There are differences, no doubt, in the taste for grilled meat from place to place around the Mediterranean. Greeks hold steadfast to the notion of well done as the only way to serve any type of meat, while the Italians, for example, have a taste for medium-rare grilled meats.

Steak, to this American-raised New Yorker, is never quite as good in the Mediterranean as it is stateside. Nevertheless, the Mediterranean has its share of great steak dishes, from the bistecca alla Florentina to the chuletas of Spain and the more humble olive oil and oregano–infused brizola, which can be either beef or pork, of Greece.

One of the favorite cuts for the grill all over the Mediterranean is the chop, either of lamb or of pork. Chops are easy to serve and versatile, able to play front and center stage at elegant dinner parties and finger-licking backyard barbecues alike.

The dishes in this chapter all beg for accompaniments. In some recipes I have offered marinades and dipping sauces as accompaniments, but almost everything in the salad, soup, and pasta chapters can be part of the meal, either as a side or as a first course to any of the meat dishes.

GRILLED BUTTERFLIED LEG OF LAMB

THIS IS by far the king of the Mediterranean grill world. The grilling process below is easy, the cut of meat accessible. You need excellent-quality lamb (I recommend organic) and good-quality, aromatic herbs to make this dish work.

MAKES 4 TO 6 SERVINGS

1 (4- to 5-pound) boned and butterflied leg of lamb

3 large garlic cloves, minced

3 tablespoons chopped fresh rosemary

3 tablespoons dried thyme, marjoram, savory, or oregano

1 tablespoon black peppercorns

1 tablespoon extra virgin olive oil

Salt to taste

2 to 3 lemons, cut in half

The butterflied leg of lamb should be about 2 inches thick. Once the butcher has butterflied it, have him pound it with a mallet to flatten to the desired thickness. (You can do this yourself, too. Place the lamb on a strong counter and bang it all over the surface with a heavy skillet or a mallet until the piece is flattened.)

Using a mortar and pestle or a spice grinder, pulverize the garlic, herbs, and peppercorns. Combine in a small bowl with the olive oil. Rub the lamb all over with the rub, pushing it into every nook and cranny in the meat, and let it rest for 1 to 2 hours or up to 6 hours.

Heat the grill to very hot.

Season the lamb with salt. Place the lamb on the hottest part of the grill (directly over the coals if you are using a charcoal grill) and sear it for about 10 minutes, turning once, to brown on all sides. Once seared, slide the lamb over to a medium-hot part of the grill and continue grilling to desired doneness, turning occasionally. Rare lamb will take about 20 minutes more, medium-rare about 25 minutes more. About halfway through grilling, cut off a tiny piece to test for doneness.

Let the meat rest for 5 minutes before slicing. Slice into 1/2-inch pieces and serve, garnished with lemon halves.

GRILLED LAMB SANDWICHES

LEFTOVER LAMB makes great sandwiches. Figure on two to three $1/8$-inch-thick slices per pita bread. Grill the pita lightly just to warm it through. For each sandwich you will need half a tomato and two $1/2$-inch round slices of a large Spanish onion, grilled.

MAKES 4 SERVINGS

2 large, firm tomatoes, cored and halved lengthwise

2 large Spanish onions, cut into $1/2$-inch round slices

4 pita breads

8 to 12 slices of leftover grilled lamb

4 tablespoons Greek-style strained yogurt, or more to taste

Cayenne pepper to taste

Freshly ground black pepper to taste

16 arugula leaves, trimmed and rinsed

Salt to taste

Heat the grill to medium-hot. Oil the grill rack.

Place the tomato halves and onion slices on the grill. Grill until lightly charred and soft, about 6 minutes, then remove. Cut the tomatoes into thin slices, reserving the juice. Warm the pita bread and lamb slices on the grill over medium heat with the lid closed for 2 to 3 minutes.

As soon as the pita and lamb are warmed through, remove from the grill. Spread the yogurt over the surface of the pita. Sprinkle with a little cayenne and black pepper. Place the lamb, onion, and tomato slices, and arugula on top. Sprinkle with salt and pepper and additional cayenne, if desired. Roll loosely to form a cylinder or fold over once to make a half-moon. Serve immediately.

GRILLED LAMB CHOPS WITH ROASTED TOMATOES AND SHEEP'S MILK CHEESE

LAMB IS undoubtedly the most popular meat in Greece, a specialty on the Easter table but also throughout the spring and summer, especially on the grill. While there are many lamb stews in Greece that call for aromatic tomato sauces or egg-lemon sauce, the best-loved way to season lamb is the simplest, with a little extra virgin Greek olive oil, garlic, and lemon juice.

MAKES 4 SERVINGS

½ cup extra virgin olive oil

½ cup fresh lemon juice

4 garlic cloves, mashed

2 tablespoons dried marjoram or oregano

1 tablespoon dried rosemary

16 lamb rib chops (two 8-rib racks), fat trimmed, cut into individual chops (about 4 pounds total)

For the tomatoes

10 large, ripe tomatoes, cored and quartered lengthwise

Salt and freshly ground black pepper to taste

1 tablespoon sugar

3 tablespoons extra virgin olive oil

3 to 4 tablespoons balsamic vinegar

Vegetable oil for brushing grill rack

4 ounces Greek kefalograviera or kefalotyri cheese, or any hard aged sheep's milk cheese

1 bunch fresh arugula, trimmed, washed, and dried for garnish

Whisk the olive oil, lemon juice, garlic, and herbs together in a medium bowl. Add the chops and toss to coat. Cover with plastic wrap and marinate in the refrigerator for at least 1 hour and up to 3 hours.

Heat the grill to hot.

Make the tomatoes: Place them in a lightly oiled shallow baking pan, skin side down. Sprinkle with salt, pepper, and the sugar and drizzle with the olive oil and the vinegar. Place on the grill rack, close the lid (make sure to leave the air vents open), and smoke the tomatoes until they are wrinkled and dried. Their edges should be slightly charred. Remove and cool.

Oil the grill rack. Remove the lamb from the marinade and pat dry. Sprinkle the lamb with salt and pepper. Raise the heat (if using gas) or shift the coals to get very hot heat. Place the lamb chops on the grill and grill to desired doneness, about 3 minutes per side for medium-rare, 4 minutes per side for medium, 5 to 6 minutes for well done. Brush with the marinade as you grill. Shave the cheese with a vegetable parer and place on a plate.

To serve, divide the tomato wedges evenly and place them in the center of four plates. As soon as the lamb comes off the grill and while it is still very hot, place it over the tomatoes and sprinkle with the cheese. Add a small cluster of arugula to each plate, drizzle with additional olive oil if desired, and serve.

THE BEST GREEK LAMB CHOPS

ALTHOUGH LAMB is one of the most popular meats of the Mediterranean, uniting rather than dividing, as the humble hog does, the Greeks stake a claim to doing it best. I have a biased opinion, of course, being of Greek descent. Certainly lamb chops on the grill with a trio of herbs, plenty of garlic, and olive oil, and, of course, lemons, are a de rigueur part of any Greek restaurant menu.

MAKES 2 TO 4 SERVINGS

**4 loin lamb chops,
about 6 ounces each**

3 large garlic cloves, minced

**2 tablespoons chopped
fresh rosemary**

1 tablespoon dried thyme

**1 tablespoon dried
savory or oregano**

1 cup dry red wine

½ cup extra virgin olive oil

**Salt and freshly ground
black pepper to taste**

2 lemons, cut in half, for garnish

Sourdough bread

Trim, rinse, and pat dry the lamb chops.

Using a spice grinder or mortar and pestle, pulverize the garlic, rosemary, thyme, and oregano. The mixture should be a paste. Rub the lamb chops all over with the herb and garlic mixture. Place in a single layer in a shallow bowl and pour in the wine and olive oil. Cover and marinate for 2 to 24 hours in the refrigerator. Let stand at room temperature for 30 minutes before grilling.

Heat the grill to hot. Season the lamb chops with salt and pepper. Grill the chops, turning once about halfway through, until desired doneness. They will need 6 to 8 minutes for rare, 8 to 10 minutes for medium, 12 to 15 minutes for well done. Serve with a lemon halves and some bread.

SPICY MOROCCAN LAMB CHOPS

LAMB IS a unifying food in the Mediterranean, one of the few meats that crosses ethnic and religious boundaries and is savored by everyone. In the eastern Mediterranean, lamb dishes tend to be seasoned with little more than garlic, lemon, and herbs; at the other end of the Mediterranean basin, more aromatic spices turn up in dry rubs, spice pastes, and marinades.

MAKES 4 SERVINGS

1 medium red onion, finely chopped

¹⁄₃ cup chopped fresh cilantro

¹⁄₂ cup chopped flat-leaf parsley

¹⁄₃ cup chopped fresh mint leaves or 2 teaspoons dried

3 garlic cloves, finely chopped

1 teaspoon ground cumin

¹⁄₂ teaspoon ground cinnamon

¹⁄₂ teaspoon ground ginger

¹⁄₂ teaspoon ground black pepper

¹⁄₂ teaspoon cayenne pepper

1 scant teaspoon sweet paprika

Strained fresh juice of 1 lemon

¹⁄₂ cup extra virgin olive oil

Salt to taste

4 loin lamb chops, about 6 ounces each, trimmed

Vegetable oil for brushing grill rack

Place the onion, cilantro, parsley, mint, and garlic in the bowl of a food processor and process until smooth. Add the cumin, cinnamon, ginger, pepper, cayenne, paprika, and lemon juice and pulse to combine. With the processor running, add the olive oil and process to a thick paste. Season, with salt, pulsing the processor once or twice to combine.

Rinse and pat dry the lamb chops. Rub both sides of the lamb chops with the spice paste and set aside to marinate for 1 hour at room temperature, covered. (You can cover and chill the marinated chops for up to 6 hours. Bring to room temperature before grilling.)

Heat the grill to hot and lightly oil the grill rack.

Place the chops on the grill and cook for about 4 minutes per side for medium-rare or 5 to 6 minutes per side for medium to well done. Remove and serve immediately.

WINE-SOAKED PORK CHOPS GLAZED WITH HONEY

YEARS AGO, while traveling through Crete, I came across a dish that called for marinating a whole pork roast in honey for days. The honey served as a tenderizer as well as a unforgettable flavoring agent. Here's is my own version of the dish.

MAKES 4 SERVINGS

³/₄ cup Greek Mavrodaphne wine or sweet Spanish Port wine

¹/₄ cup dry red wine

¹/₄ cup extra virgin olive oil

3 garlic cloves, finely chopped

3 tablespoons chopped fresh oregano or marjoram

1 tablespoon balsamic vinegar

1 scant teaspoon freshly ground black pepper

4 (³/₄-inch-thick) loin pork chops, trimmed

Vegetable oil for brushing grill rack

¹/₂ teaspoon salt

2 tablespoons honey

Stir together the wines, olive oil, garlic, oregano, balsamic vinegar, and pepper. Score the edges of each chop in a few places to keep from curling on the grill. Place the pork chops in a shallow glass or ceramic baking tray and pour the marinade over them. Cover with plastic wrap and marinate for 2 hours in the refrigerator. Bring to room temperature 30 minutes before grilling.

Heat the grill to very hot and lightly oil a grill rack.

Remove the chops from the marinade with a slotted spoon and place on the grill directly over the hottest part or over glowing coals. Grill for 2 minutes on each side, then move to a cooler part of the grill or lower the heat slightly. Stir the salt and honey into the marinade. Brush over the pork chops continuously and grill for 4 to 5 minutes per side. Remove, rest the chops on a serving platter for a few minutes, and serve.

SPANISH-STYLE GRILLED PORK CHOPS

WHAT LAMB is to the Greeks, pork is to the Spanish, and this simple dish illustrates the seasonings that are most prevalent in the grilled pork dishes of Spain.

MAKES 4 SERVINGS

4 (³⁄₄-inch-thick) loin pork chops

4 large garlic cloves

1 tablespoon fresh oregano leaves

1 tablespoon paprika

2 teaspoons cayenne pepper or hot paprika or red pepper flakes, or less to taste

Salt and freshly ground black pepper to taste

¹⁄₂ cup dry white wine

¹⁄₄ cup extra virgin olive oil

Vegetable oil for brushing grill rack

Rinse and trim the pork chops. Score the edges of each chop in a few places to keep it from curling up on the grill.

Mash the garlic cloves to a paste with the flat side of a large knife or press through a garlic press. Combine the garlic, oregano, paprika, cayenne, and salt and pepper and rub this mixture into the pork chops. Leave in a shallow plate, covered and refrigerated, for 1 hour.

Pour in the wine and olive oil, turn once, and marinate, covered and refrigerated, for at least 2 and up to 24 hours. Let stand at room temperature for 30 minutes before grilling.

Heat the grill to hot and brush the grill rack with oil.

Grill the chops directly over the coals or over the hottest part of the grill for 3 minutes per side, turning. Slide the chops over to a cooler part of the grill or over the part of the rack with no coals underneath (if using a gas grill adjust the heat to medium-hot), and continue grilling for another 4 minutes per side, or until cooked through. Remove to a platter, cover, and let sit for 3 to 5 minutes before serving.

FENNEL-PEPPER PORK CHOPS

THIS RECIPE takes its flavor profile from the Italian love affair with fennel and pork.

MAKES 4 SERVINGS

4 (³/₄-inch-thick) loin pork chops

1 heaping tablespoon fennel seeds

1 heaping teaspoon red pepper flakes

¹/₄ cup extra virgin olive oil

Salt to taste

Vegetable oil for brushing grill rack

Trim the excess fat off the chops. Place on a cutting board, place a piece of plastic wrap over them, and pound slightly with a kitchen mallet to flatten to about ¹/₂ inch.

Grind the fennel seeds and red pepper flakes in a spice grinder or in a small mortar with a pestle. Combine with the olive oil and season with salt. Rub the chops with this mixture and set aside, covered, in a shallow pan for 30 minutes.

Heat a grill to hot and brush the grill rack with oil.

Grill the chops directly over the coals or over the hottest part of the grill for 2 minutes per side, turning. Slide the chops over to a cooler part of the grill or over the part of the rack with no coals underneath (if using a gas grill, adjust the heat to medium-hot), and continue grilling for another 3 minutes per side, or until cooked through. Remove to a platter, cover, and let sit for 3 to 5 minutes before serving.

GRILLED PORK CHOPS STUFFED WITH FETA AND OLIVES

GREEK MEETS grill in this easy, filling dish.

MAKES 4 SERVINGS

Vegetable oil for
brushing grill rack

4 (³/₄-inch-thick) loin
pork chops

1¹/₂ cups crumbled
Greek feta

4 tablespoons chopped pitted
Greek green olives

2 tablespoons grated lemon zest

4 tablespoons chopped
fresh mint

Freshly ground
black pepper to taste

2 to 3 tablespoons olive oil

Salt to taste

2 to 3 lemons, cut in half
lengthwise, for garnish

Heat the grill to hot and oil the grill rack.

Make a pocketlike slit on the flesh side of each pork chop and score the fat on the outer side of the chop so it doesn't curl up when grilling.

Using a fork, mash together the feta, olives, lemon zest, and mint. Season with a little pepper. Fill each pork chop with a quarter of the feta mixture. Press closed. Lightly oil each pork chop and place on the grill. Grill for about 7 minutes per side, brushing as needed with a little oil. Salt on both sides, remove from the grill, and let stand for a minute or two. Serve with lemon juice squeezed over and garnished with a lemon half.

ORANGE-HONEY GRILLED PORK TENDERLOIN

HONEY, ORANGE, mustard, and vinegar are a timeless quartet, enhancing all sorts of dishes, from salad dressings to sautéed seafood to this grilled pork tenderloin.

MAKES 4 SERVINGS

⅓ cup strained fresh orange juice

⅓ cup honey, preferably Greek thyme or pine honey

3 tablespoons sherry vinegar

3 tablespoons Dijon mustard

1 (2-pound) pork tenderloin, trimmed

Vegetable oil for brushing grill rack

Salt and freshly ground black pepper to taste

In a medium bowl, whisk the orange juice, honey, vinegar, and mustard until smooth. Pour the marinade into a large, resealable plastic bag and add the pork tenderloin. Seal and refrigerate for at least 4 and up to 24 hours.

Heat the grill to medium-hot and lightly oil the grill rack.

Remove the pork from the marinade and wipe dry. Season the pork with salt and pepper and reserve the marinade. Grill the pork, turning and brushing with the marinade, for about 20 minutes, or until cooked through. Let the tenderloin rest for a few minutes before serving.

While the pork is resting, pour the marinade into a small skillet and bring to a boil over medium heat. Reduce the heat and simmer for 1 to 2 minutes, until the marinade thickens to a loose, syrupy consistency. Remove. Thinly slice the pork, pour over the sauce, and serve.

GRILLED PORK TENDERLOIN WITH OUZO-PLUM GLAZE

IN OUR backyard in Ikaria we have three old, lumbering plum trees. Each year they provide us with plums to savor raw, plums for jams, jellies, spoon sweets, and chutneys, and other recipes that evolve on a lark, based on what happens to be on hand on a given day in my summer cupboard. This is one of them.

MAKES 4 SERVINGS

3 tablespoons olive oil

½ cup strained fresh orange juice

2 tablespoons sherry vinegar

1 (2-pound) pork tenderloin, trimmed

For the glaze

2 cups coarsely chopped fresh pitted prune plums or damson plums

½ cup sugar

⅔ cup ouzo or other anise-flavored liqueur

3 tablespoons extra virgin olive oil

1 large red onion, finely chopped

⅓ cup strained fresh orange juice

4 tablespoons balsamic vinegar

4 fresh sage leaves, finely chopped

2 bay leaves, cracked

4 whole cloves

Salt and freshly ground black pepper to taste

Vegetable oil for brushing grill rack

Whisk together the olive oil, orange juice, and sherry vinegar in a small bowl and pour the mixture into a resealable plastic bag. Place the tenderloin in the bag, turn to coat, seal, and refrigerate for 2 hours.

In the meantime, make the glaze: Place the plums, sugar, and ouzo in a large bowl and let marinate, covered, at room temperature, for 1 hour.

Heat the olive oil in a medium saucepan over medium heat and sauté the onion until soft and lightly colored, about 12 minutes. Add the plums and their juices as well as the orange juice, balsamic vinegar, sage, bay leaves, and cloves. Bring to a boil over high heat. Reduce the heat to medium-low, season with salt and pepper, and cook the sauce uncovered for 35 to 40 minutes, or until it is very thick and jamlike in consistency. Remove the bay leaves and cloves. Transfer the sauce to the bowl of a food processor and purée until very smooth. There will be more glaze than needed for the recipe; save the remainder in a lidded jar in the refrigerator or serve with the pork, as well as with other grilled meats, almost like a chutney.

Heat the grill to medium and lightly oil the grill rack.

Remove the pork from the marinade and wipe dry. Season generously with salt and pepper. Place on the grill, and cook for about 10 minutes per side, turning every 4 to 5 minutes. Brush with the glaze during the last 6 to 7 minutes of grilling. Remove, let rest for a few minutes, and serve accompanied by the plum glaze.

BISTECCA ALLA FLORENTINA

TWO THINGS make for a great grilled steak: the meat itself and the skill of the person doing the grilling, a skill acquired through experience. Real Florentine steak is made with real Florentine beef—namely, from massive oxen raised near Arezzo in the Chiana Valley. A typical Florentine steak is huge—around 5 or 6 pounds—and is meant to be shared among several diners. The cut closest to what the Florentines savor is a porterhouse, aged well.

MAKES 2 SERVINGS

1 aged (2-inch-thick) porterhouse, 2 to 2½ pounds

Salt and freshly ground black pepper to taste

Heat the grill to very hot (a charcoal grill is really best for steaks).

Place the steak on the grill and sear it. You don't want grill marks on this steak. As soon as it sears on one side, flip the steak and season it generously with salt and pepper. Grill for 8 to 9 minutes, or until the steak comes off the grill easily. Flip it again, salt and pepper the other side and keep it on the grill another 3 to 4 minutes. For a medium-rare porterhouse, the average cooking time is a total of about 9 minutes per side. Remove and let it stand for 5 minutes. Cut the steak on an angle into ¼-inch slices and serve.

Variation: Season the steak with garlic and serve it topped with arugula and shaved Parmesan cheese, which is how it is served in some Italian restaurants throughout North America. Using a mortar and pestle or small food processor, make a paste of 4 garlic cloves, 1 tablespoon extra virgin olive oil, and 1 scant teaspoon freshly ground black pepper. Rub this mixture on both sides of the steak and let it stand, covered and at room temperature, for 30 minutes. Grill on a hot grill for about 9 minutes on one side, then flip and season with salt. Grill the second side for another 8 to 9 minutes, flip, salt, and remove. Let it stand for 5 minutes, then cut into ¼-inch slices. Serve on a grooved platter to capture all the juices exuded when the steak is cut. Top the sliced steak with ¼ pound of trimmed fresh arugula leaves and about 2 ounces of Parmesan, shaved. Drizzle with a little olive oil and serve.

CHULETAS WITH ROQUEFORT BUTTER

THIS SPANISH CLASSIC grilled T-bone is usually adorned with a melting dollop of blue Cabrales cheese mashed with butter. I use Roquefort because it's easier to find.

MAKES 4 SERVINGS

4 tablespoons (½ stick)
unsalted butter,
at room temperature

½ cup crumbled Roquefort or
other blue cheese,
at room temperature

Sea salt and freshly ground
black pepper to taste

Vegetable oil for brushing
grill rack

4 (12-ounce) T-bone steaks

2 tablespoons extra virgin
olive oil

Mash the butter and cheese together with a fork and season with salt and pepper. Shape into a log about 3 inches long and wrap tight in plastic. Refrigerate until firm enough to slice, about 1 hour.

Heat the grill to hot and oil the grill rack.

Season the steaks generously with pepper and olive oil and grill until desired doneness, about 5 minutes per side for medium-rare. About a minute before removing from the grill, season generously with salt. Serve the steaks on individual plates or on a platter and garnish each with a tablespoon of the Roquefort butter.

ROSEMARY VEAL CHOPS ON THE GRILL

MAKES 6 SERVINGS

**2 tablespoons fresh
rosemary leaves**

2 garlic cloves, peeled

**Salt and freshly ground black
pepper to taste**

$\frac{1}{2}$ cup extra virgin olive oil

$\frac{1}{2}$ cup dry red wine

6 veal chops, 8 ounces each

Using a mortar and pestle or spice grinder, pound the rosemary, garlic, salt, and pepper to a paste. Whisk the olive oil and wine together in a small bowl and add the herb paste.

Rinse and pat dry the veal chops. Place in a shallow bowl with the marinade, turn to coat, cover, and let stand at room temperature for 1 hour. (You can refrigerate for up to 24 hours, but bring the meat to room temperature before grilling.)

Heat the grill to medium-hot.

Remove the chops from the marinade and place on the grill. Grill for about 4 minutes per side for medium-rare, 5 minutes per side for medium, and 6 to 7 minutes per side for well done. Season each side with salt and pepper, and serve.

WINGS
afire

When I first moved to Greece, as a young freelance journalist in the early 1980s, take-out food was just beginning to be popular. The favorite quick family meal at the time (besides pizza, which was still a novelty) was rotisserie chicken. In residential neighborhoods in all the major cities, grilled chicken places are still popular take-out shops, rows and rows of glistening whole birds turn on automated spits; the aroma of lemon and oregano—typical Greek seasonings—wafting through apartment house corridors all evening long.

Chicken is one of the most versatile foods, on and off the grill. It responds well to such a vast array of flavors and cooking techniques that it is no wonder chicken is arguably the world's most popular "meat." Grilled chicken is a classic in almost every culture, a mirror of regional tastes, from the Greek lemon-oregano duet to the aromatic spiced chickens grilled in Moroccan tradition and the honey-marinated grilled chickens that the Spanish love so much.

The mild flavor of chicken enables it to marry well with all sorts of marinade, from alcohol-based brews with grappa and wine to citrus and yogurt baths. And, of course, because of its fatty skin, which keeps the chicken succulent when charred, it is perfect for either direct or indirect heat of the grill.

Other poultry, too, has fat on its side when it comes to grilling, especially duck. Delicate quail require the cook's full attention because of their small size, but they are delicious marinated and grilled, their gamy flavor enhanced by the aromas of the coal- or wood-fired barbecue.

Inspired by the capacity of poultry and fowl to stand up so well to so many different things, I offer a more extensive and varied range of flavors and marinades in this chapter than elsewhere in this book. Grilled poultry, no matter how it's seasoned, is classic in the Mediterranean and beyond.

GREEK LEMONY MARINATED GRILLED SPLIT CHICKEN

ALL OVER GREECE, the heady, tangy scents of grilled chicken, usually done on a rotisserie, waft through every neighborhood. Grilled chicken is classic take-out fare and something one finds in tavernas all over the country. The typical accompaniment to this dish is Greek potatoes fried in olive oil and a tomato salad. Also try it with Grilled Sweet Potatoes and Leeks (page 36) or with Grilled Late Summer Squash (page 30).

MAKES 4 SERVINGS

½ cup extra virgin olive oil

½ cup strained fresh lemon juice

⅓ cup dry white wine

4 garlic cloves, minced

½ cup chopped fresh oregano leaves

1 scant teaspoon freshly ground black pepper

1 (3½-pound) whole chicken, giblets removed, split in half

Vegetable oil for brushing grill rack

Salt to taste

In a large bowl, whisk together the olive oil, lemon juice, wine, and garlic until smooth and emulsified. Mix in the oregano and pepper. Turn the chicken in the marinade, cover, and refrigerate for 2 hours or up to 8 hours. Remove from the refrigerator and bring to room temperature in the marinade. Remove from the marinade and pat dry.

Heat the grill to medium-hot and brush the grill rack with oil.

Place the chicken on the grill skin side down, and sear for 6 to 7 minutes. Salt, then turn and sear on the other side. Salt again. Brush and turn the chicken every 7 to 8 minutes or so, for a total of 35 to 40 minutes, brushing occasionally with the marinade, until the chicken is tender on the inside and crisp on the outside. Remove, cut into portions, and serve.

MOROCCAN GRILLED CHICKEN

CUMIN, CORIANDER, and a touch of cinnamon give this dish its Moroccan spirit.

MAKES 4 TO 6 SERVINGS

3 tablespoons cumin seeds

2 tablespoons coriander seeds

1 tablespoon ground cinnamon

1 scant tablespoon salt

1 to 2 teaspoons sugar

1/2 to 1 scant teaspoon cayenne pepper

Freshly ground black pepper to taste

1 1/4 cups extra virgin olive oil

1/3 cup red wine vinegar

4 chicken breast halves, with bones and skin

3 pounds chicken legs and thighs, separated, skin on

Grind the cumin and coriander seeds in a mortar with a pestle or in a spice grinder. Mix in a small bowl with the cinnamon, salt, sugar, cayenne, and pepper. In a large stainless steel or glass bowl, whisk together the olive oil, vinegar, and spice mix until smooth and emulsified.

Cut the chicken breasts in half horizontally. Toss the breasts, legs, and thighs in the marinade, turning to coat well on all sides. Cover with plastic wrap and leave to marinate in the refrigerate for 2 to 8 hours. Turn occasionally in the marinade.

Heat the grill to medium.

Remove the chicken pieces from the marinade with a slotted spoon and place on the grill. Grill until done, 10 to 12 minutes per side for the breasts and 12 to 14 minutes per side for the legs and thighs. Turn once as you grill and brush occasionally with the marinade. Place the grilled chicken on a platter and serve.

GLAZED CHICKEN BREASTS OVER COOKED GREENS

PETIMEZI, OR PETMEZ, a traditional syrup found in the eastern Mediterranean, is made from boiled-down grape must at the time of the harvest, from mid-August through late September. It has a lovely, rich, dense, and almost spicy flavor. I use it here to create a Mediterranean barbecue sauce with orange juice, a little red wine vinegar, and pepper. You can find petmez in gourmet shops as well as in Greek and Middle Eastern food stores. Serve the glazed, grilled chicken breasts with a simple green salad or with boiled greens, called *horta* in Greece.

MAKES 6 SERVINGS

3 large juice oranges, such as Temple

½ cup balsamic vinegar

¼ cup red wine vinegar

½ cup petmez

4 large garlic cloves, minced

1 teaspoon salt

1 tablespoon Turkish spicy red pepper paste or hot sauce

1 scant teaspoon freshly ground black pepper

6 chicken breast halves, boned but with skin on

Wash the oranges very well. Grate them along the fine side of a cheese grater or with a zester. Reserve 3 tablespoons of the grated rind and discard the rest or save for another use. Juice the oranges. You should get about 1½ cups.

Combine the orange juice, vinegars, petmez, garlic, salt, grated orange zest, hot pepper paste, and pepper in a medium bowl. Place the chicken in the marinade and turn. Cover with plastic wrap and refrigerate for at least 3 hours or up to 24 hours, turning occasionally.

Heat the grill to medium-hot.

For the horta

3 pounds dandelion or chard greens, trimmed

¹/₂ cup extra virgin olive oil, or more as needed

2 tablespoons red wine vinegar

Salt to taste

Make the horta: Bring a large pot of salted water to a boil and drop in the greens. Place the cover ajar over the pot and bring the greens to a boil over high heat. Reduce the heat to medium and simmer until the greens are tender, about 20 minutes. Remove and drain well.

Meanwhile, remove the chicken from the marinade with a slotted spoon, allowing as much as possible of the marinade to drip back into the bowl. Whisk the marinade again and pour half of it into a small saucepan. Bring to a boil, reduce the heat, and simmer until it is as thick as syrup, 5 to 6 minutes. Set aside.

Blot the chicken dry with paper towels and transfer to the grill. Grill for 8 to 9 minutes per side, or until cooked through and browned on the outside. Brush with the marinade during the last 3 to 4 minutes of grilling. Remove the chicken to a serving platter. Place the horta in a serving bowl, season with the olive oil, vinegar, and salt. Serve with the chicken and pass around the petmez sauce.

SMOKED SPANISH-STYLE GRILLED CHICKEN

HONEY AND CUMIN make for an intoxicating duet of aromas and flavors. This dish speaks of the sweet-and-sour Moorish influences that prevail in so much Spanish food.

MAKES 4 SERVINGS

1 whole broiler chicken, about 3 pounds, trimmed

¼ cup olive oil, plus more as needed

2 to 3 tablespoons sherry vinegar, plus more as needed

2 garlic cloves, very finely chopped

1 tablespoon ground cumin

Salt and freshly ground black pepper to taste

3 tablespoons honey

Trim the back from the chicken. Remove the giblets packet and set aside for another use. Wash the chicken inside and out and pat dry.

In a large, shallow bowl, whisk together the olive oil and vinegar. Mix in the garlic, cumin, salt, and pepper. Place the chicken in the bowl and turn to coat all over with the marinade. Cover, refrigerate, and marinate for 1 to 4 hours, turning every now and then in the marinade.

Heat the grill to medium.

Place the chicken breast side up on a rack in a shallow roasting pan. Generously brush the breast, thighs, and wings with marinade. Place the pan on the grill rack. Cover the grill (make sure the vents are open) and smoke the chicken for 1¼ to 1¾ hours. During the course of cooking, brush the chicken every 10 or 15 minutes with the marinade. About 15 to 20 minutes before the chicken is cooked, whisk the honey into the marinade and replenish with a little olive oil and vinegar. Brush this all over the chicken. Continue grilling until the chicken is a deep brown with a crisp skin and is cooked all the way through, about 10 more minutes. Remove the chicken from the grill, cover with aluminum foil to keep warm, and let it rest for 10 minutes before carving.

GRILLED GRAPPA-CITRUS CHICKEN

GRAPPA, OR the Greek equivalent, tsipouro, lends a subtle, wine-like undertone to this dish. It is a common component in marinades and sauces in Italy and Greece. This goes really well with the Tabouleh with Arugula (page 10) or with the Chickpea Salad with Grilled Eggplant (page 11).

MAKES 6 SERVINGS

½ cup extra virgin olive oil

½ cup fresh grapefruit juice

½ cup fresh lemon juice

½ cup fresh orange juice

½ cup Greek tsipouro (eau de vie) or Italian grappa

2 small red chili peppers, seeded and minced

1 large garlic clove, minced or pressed

½ cup finely chopped fresh mint leaves

1 teaspoon salt

1 teaspoon freshly ground black pepper

6 chicken breast halves, boned but with skin on

Vegetable oil for brushing grill rack

In a large glass or stainless steel bowl, whisk together the olive oil, grapefruit, lemon, and orange juices, tsipouro or grappa, chili peppers, garlic, mint, salt, and pepper. Add the chicken breasts and turn in the marinade to coat. Cover with plastic wrap and refrigerate for 4 to 24 hours. Turn occasionally in the marinade.

Heat the grill to medium-hot and brush the rack with oil.

Remove the chicken from the marinade and blot dry with paper towels. Transfer to the grill. Grill for 8 to 9 minutes per side or until cooked through, turning once. Brush with the marinade during the last 5 to 6 minutes of grilling. Serve.

GRILLED CHICKEN BREASTS WITH ROQUEFORT AND DRIED FIGS

RICH AND filling, this dish is great with something simple, such as mashed potatoes, steamed rice, or a green salad.

MAKES 4 SERVINGS

4 chicken breast halves, boned but not skinned

For the marinade

1 small cinnamon stick

4 or 5 whole cloves

4 or 5 allspice berries

Freshly ground black pepper to taste

1 cup Greek Mavrodaphne wine, Port, or sweet Marsala wine

¹⁄₂ cup fresh orange juice

¹⁄₂ cup extra virgin olive oil

Vegetable oil for brushing grill rack

¹⁄₂ cup sugar

¹⁄₃ cup balsamic vinegar

6 large, plump dried figs (see Note)

¹⁄₂ cup crumbled Roquefort or other sharp blue cheese

2 tablespoons brandy

Using a sharp paring knife and starting at the thick end of each breast, make a lengthwise incision to form a pocket. Make the pocket as wide as possible without ripping through the breast.

Make the marinade: Lightly pound the cinnamon stick, cloves, allspice, and pepper in a small mortar with a pestle. In a large stainless steel or glass bowl, whisk together the wine, orange juice, and olive oil. Add the crushed spices. Place the breasts in the marinade, turn to coat, cover with plastic wrap, and refrigerate for at least 2 hours or up to 8 hours. Turn occasionally in the marinade.

Heat the grill to medium and brush the grill racks with oil.

Remove the chicken breasts and set aside until ready to fill. Place the marinade, sugar, and vinegar in a small saucepan, bring to a boil over high heat, lower the heat to medium, and simmer until the mixture is reduced to about 1 cup and thick, almost syrupy, about 45 minutes. Remove and set aside.

Cut the figs in half. Mash the Roquefort, pepper to taste, and brandy in a small bowl and fill each fig half with a little bit of the mixture, pressing it in. Squeeze three fig halves into each of the slit chicken breasts and press closed or secure closed with small metal skewers.

Place the chicken breasts on the grill. After 10 to 12 minutes, begin brushing with some of the syrupy marinade. Grill, brushing every few minutes, for a total of 20 to 25 minutes, turning once or twice, until the outside of the chicken is dark and caramelized and the breasts are cooked through. Serve.

NOTE: It's really important to use plump, juicy dried figs. Avoid figs that have crystallized on the outside or that are exceedingly tough.

GRILLED CHICKEN LEGS WITH TOMATO-OLIVE BARBECUE SAUCE

MY FRIEND Aris Kefalogiannis, owner of Gaea Foods, came out with an olive marmalade that was the brainchild of one of Greece's best-known pastry chefs. Since it's not readily available in North America, I took the idea and combined olive paste, tomato paste, honey, and more to create to barbecue sauce with Mediterranean identity.

MAKES 6 SERVINGS

1/3 cup extra virgin olive oil, plus 3 tablespoons for brushing pita

2 large red onions, finely chopped

2 garlic cloves, finely chopped

1/2 cup red wine vinegar

1/3 cup Greek raisin vinegar or balsamic vinegar

1 cup tomato purée

1/4 cup tomato paste

1/3 cup Kalamata olive paste

1/2 cup honey

1 tablespoon Worcestershire

4 tablespoons steak sauce

3 tablespoons ouzo, Sambuca, or other anise-flavored liqueur

Salt and freshly ground black pepper to taste

Vegetable oil for brushing grill rack

6 whole chicken legs and thighs, skin on, trimmed of excess fat

6 pita breads

In a medium saucepan, heat the 1/3 cup olive oil over medium heat and add the onions. Reduce heat, cover, and sweat in the oil for about 10 minutes, stirring occasionally so as not to burn. Add the garlic and stir for another 3 to 4 minutes. Pour in the vinegars, tomato purée, tomato paste, olive paste, honey, Worcestershire sauce, steak sauce, ouzo, and salt and pepper. Raise the heat to high and bring to a boil. Reduce the heat and simmer for 10 to 12 minutes, until the mixture is a little thicker than ketchup. Remove from the heat, divide, and transfer to two small bowls, and let cool.

Heat the grill to medium-hot and oil the grill rack.

Brush the chicken generously on all sides with the barbecue sauce. (Use the one reserved bowl for later as a dipping sauce for the grilled chicken.) Place skin side down on the hottest part of the grill, turn once, and sear on both sides for 5 to 7 minutes. Make sure all the chicken is skin side up as you shift the pieces to a cooler part of the grill rack. Cover the barbecue with its lid and cook the chicken for 25 to 35 minutes, turning and basting every 8 to 10 minutes with the barbecue sauce, until the chicken is cooked through, tender on the inside, and dark and crisp on the outside. Transfer to a serving platter.

Brush each pita with 1/2 tablespoon olive oil and grill for a few minutes, turning once, until the pita is lined with grill marks. Serve immediately together with the chicken.

SWEET TOMATO-GLAZED DUCK BREASTS

GREEKS MAKE spoon sweets, essentially syrup preserves, from almost every seasonal fruit, some whole nuts, and a few vegetables. *Tomataki glyko*, as this sweet is called in Greek, is a preserve of small, usually whole tomatoes. It makes a great and unusual glaze, coupled with some newer additions to the Greek kitchen, such as ginger. The glazed duck goes very well with mashed potatoes.

MAKES 8 SERVINGS

1 cup Greek tomato spoon sweet (see Note)

½ cup dry white wine

½ cup strained fresh orange juice

3 rose geranium leaves or 4 fresh sage leaves

2 teaspoons finely chopped fresh ginger

1 (2 × ½-inch) piece lemon zest

Freshly ground black pepper

½ teaspoon red pepper flakes

Salt

4 whole boneless duck breasts, with skin, cut in half

Strain the tomato spoon sweet. Reserve the syrup and purée the tomato in a food processor until smooth. Place the puréed tomato, syrup, wine, orange juice, rose geranium, ginger, and lemon zest in a medium saucepan and bring to a boil over high heat. Reduce the heat and simmer until the mixture is reduced to 1½ cups. Add 1 scant teaspoon black pepper, the red pepper flakes, and a pinch of salt.

With a sharp paring knife, score the skin of each duck breast in a crisscross fashion. Season the breasts with salt and pepper and brush on both sides with a little of the glaze. Place in a shallow pan or baking dish, cover with plastic wrap, and refrigerate for at least 2 hours and up to 8 hours. Set the remaining glaze aside, covered.

Heat the grill to medium-hot. Remove the duck from the refrigerator, allow to stand for 30 minutes or until at room temperature, then place skin side down on the grill. Grill for 1 to 2 minutes, just to caramelize the surface. Use a water sprayer to extinguish any flames that flare up from the duck fat drippings. Remove the breasts from the grill and transfer, skin side down, to a shallow pan. Place back on the grill rack, close the lid, and smoke the duck for 8 to 10 minutes for rare, 10 to 12 minutes for medium. Open the lid and brush occasionally with the glaze as you do this.

Remove the duck and let rest a few minutes, covered with an aluminum foil tent to keep warm. Slice into thin diagonal pieces and serve with the extra glaze on the side as a dipping sauce.

NOTE: Tomato spoon sweet can be found in Greek and Middle Eastern food shops. You can substitute with orange spoon sweet or orange marmalade.

GRILLED QUAIL

MY FAVORITE way to serve delicate quail is with a fresh fava bean purée, which is easy to make by cleaning and boiling young spring fava beans, and mashing or whipping them in a food processor with plenty of good olive oil, salt, pepper, lemon juice, and a pinch of sugar. I like to serve this with Tabbouleh with Grilled Asparagus, Mint, and Pine Nuts (page 13).

MAKES 4 SERVINGS

8 boneless quail

½ cup extra virgin olive oil

1 cup fresh orange juice

½ cup fresh lemon juice

½ cup white wine

5 garlic cloves, crushed

2 tablespoons fresh rosemary, pounded to a paste

1 scant teaspoon salt

2 teaspoons crushed pink peppercorns

Split the quail in half lengthwise from the backbone without separating the two halves. Remove any viscera.

In a large bowl, whisk together the olive oil, orange and lemon juices, white wine, garlic, rosemary, salt, and pink peppercorns. Place the quail in the bowl, toss to coat with the marinade, cover with plastic wrap, and refrigerate for 2 hours or up to 24 hours.

Heat the grill to medium. Place the quail opened side down on the grill. Brush with the marinade every minute or so and grill, turning, for about 4 minutes per side, until done. The quail should be light pink on the inside. Remove and serve.

GRILLED QUAIL
WITH FENNEL-CARROT-RAISIN SLAW

THE HONEY-SWEET and sour-vinegar motifs that run through so much Mediterranean cooking trace their roots both to ancient flavor combinations and to Moorrish-Ottoman influences. This dish is both new and old, with the slaw adding a decidedly backyard-America flavor to the heady, almost Eastern aromas in the quail.

MAKES 4 SERVINGS

½ cup raspberry vinegar

½ cup honey, preferably Greek pine or thyme honey

⅔ cup olive oil

½ heaping teaspoon freshly grated nutmeg

½ teaspoon ground allspice

Salt and freshly ground black pepper to taste

8 boneless quail

For the slaw

3 tablespoons raspberry or cider vinegar

1 tablespoon honey

¼ cup extra virgin olive oil

1 large fennel bulb, trimmed and finely sliced

2 large carrots, grated

1 small red onion, thinly sliced

1 small garlic clove, minced

3 tablespoons golden raisins

½ teaspoon coarsely ground fennel seeds

1 teaspoon roasted sesame seeds or nigella seeds

In a large bowl, whisk together the vinegar, honey, olive oil, spices, 1 teaspoon salt, and 1 scant teaspoon pepper. Rinse and pat dry the quail. Place in the marinade and toss to coat. Cover with plastic wrap and marinate for at least 2 hours and up to 24 hours.

Make the slaw: In a small bowl, whisk together the vinegar, honey, olive oil, salt, and pepper. Toss the shredded fennel bulb, carrots, onion, and garlic together in a serving bowl. Add the raisins, pour in the dressing, and toss to mix well. Sprinkle with fennel and sesame seeds.

Heat the grill to medium. About 30 minutes before grilling, remove the quail from the refrigerator and bring to room temperature in the marinade.

Remove the quail from the marinade and wipe dry. Save the marinade for basting. Grill the quail, turning, over medium-high heat, for 4 to 6 minutes on each side, brushing occasionally with the marinade. Remove from the grill and set aside, covered, to keep warm.

Divide the slaw into four portions and serve two quail over each portion on separate plates, or all together on a serving platter.

SURF
on turf

It's dawn in the northeastern Aegean and I have taken a group of adventurous Americans down to a small port called Yialiskari on the island of Ikaria, where we are about to embark on an hours-long fishing expedition. The sea is a stretched silk surface as smooth and blue as lapis, and the sun in the early morning is a resounding pink.

We set out on a professional fishing boat outfitted with pulleys and nets and teetering antennae and with two leather-faced fishermen with cigarettes glued to their lips, all in the name of having some fun. In hand, we balance a couple of coffees and try to find a place to lean among the labyrinth of gear scattered all over the deck. Suddenly, ten, twelve, maybe more, onyx-colored dolphins arc and slice through the water—aquatic Baryshnikovs. Even the fishermen stop to savor the moment.

The Mediterranean is the life-giver in every corner of the basin—a constant, as sure as day, feeding commerce and existing as the backdrop to that most beloved Mediterranean entertainment, people watching. Merry colored boats bob in the water, passersby strut on their daily promenades, fishermen unload and untangle their nets, waiters swirl trays of everything from coffee to tiny golden-grilled fish. The Mediterranean is a sea of nourishment for body and soul.

Its bounty has been savored from time immemorial, from the ancient Greeks who waxed poetic on the provenance and character of specific fishes, to the present-day Tunisians who still fish for tuna the way their ancestors have for centuries, to the ultra-modern fishing boats that flash-freeze their catch so that it arrives as vibrant and flavorful as possible in fish markets the world over. It's a sea for which the seasons play out like talismans, indelibly forecasting the possibilities at the table. Oily fish like tuna and mackerel in summer; shellfish never in months where there is no "R"—a common kitchen canon in Greece; fresh squid in August. Like clockwork all over the Mediterranean, traditional cooks still abide by the sea's calendar of treats, but overfishing and pollution have played their menacing roles in depleting what was once a sea bursting with life.

Where does the grill figure in all of this? Prominently, for nothing is more quintessentially Mediterranean than a glistening platter of fish or seafood, awash in the ablutions of olive oil and herbs, radiating with the woody aroma of charcoal, each plate a sea of textural and sensory contradictions: crisp but tender and sweet but slightly charred in the case of fish; tough but succulent in the case of a perfectly grilled octopus or squid.

In the recipes that follow I have tried to bring the Mediterranean's ease of preparation and wealth of flavors home to the American cook. The dishes are easy, immediate, and vibrant.

147

GRILLED WHOLE FISH

THERE ISN'T exactly a recipe for grilled whole fish but rather a technique that applies to all fish suitable for grilling. That includes a wide range of fish. Only very small fish are not so suitable for the grill because they tend to fall apart. But sea bass, grouper, snappers, large red mullets, whole small cod, bream, shad, even bony rock fish usually savored in soups are excellent on the grill.

First, clean the fish. Scrape off its scales with a sharp paring knife, running it against the grain of the scales so that they come right off. Gut the fish, cutting its underside and removing all viscera. Heat the grill to medium-hot and oil both the grill rack and basket. Grilling directly on the grill rack can be risky, especially when the fish needs to be turned. Its flesh is usually so tender that the fish falls apart. A long-handled grill basket is very useful when grilling whole fish because the fish is secured within and stays together.

My favorite way to serve and savor grilled fish is the simplest: with a small bowl of extra virgin olive oil and lemon juice whisked together with a little salt, pepper, and fresh oregano. I use this to brush on the fish as it grills and also serve it with the fish, drizzling it over the flesh as soon as I cut open the fish and debone it. You can use the not-so-classic olive oil and lemon dressing on page 165 to accompany and flavor your grilled fish; or using the same proportions of olive oil to lemon juice, omit the saffron and replace it with 2 tablespoons of chopped fresh oregano leaves.

SIMPLE GRILLED TUNA

THERE IS nothing worse than overcooked fresh tuna and nothing better than a perfectly grilled tuna steak. When its surface is seared and its interior rose colored and slightly translucent, tuna is perfect. And grilling tuna is the best way to prepare the fish. The fewer embellishments the better. Fresh tuna needs little else besides a rubbing of olive oil, salt, and pepper. This dish goes really well with the Tabbouleh with Arugula, Grilled Onions, Orange, and Red Pepper (page 10).

You can use this same technique for grilling other thick fish steaks, such as swordfish, halibut, and salmon.

MAKES 4 SERVINGS

Vegetable oil for brushing grill rack

4 (10-ounce) boneless tuna steaks

4 tablespoons extra virgin olive oil

Salt and freshly ground black pepper to taste

Heat the grill to hot. Oil the grill rack.

Rub each tuna steak with 1 tablespoon olive oil and season on both sides with salt and pepper. Place the tuna steaks on the rack. Grill for 3 to 4 minutes per side. To check for doneness, bend the tuna a little using a pair of tongs. The center should still be pinkish and translucent. Remove and serve.

GRILLED SARDINES WITH ONION RINGS AND HERBS

SARDINES, with their earthy, ruddy flavors, do quite well on the grill. The fish, despite their small size, are oily enough so as not to dry out when grilled with care.

MAKES 4 SERVINGS

¹/₃ cup extra virgin olive oil

¹/₃ cup strained fresh lemon juice

1 teaspoon dried oregano, preferably Greek

Salt and white pepper to taste

1 pound fresh sardines, gutted but whole

Vegetable oil for brushing grill basket

2 large red onions, peeled and sliced into paper-thin rings

1 teaspoon sweet paprika or a combination of sweet and hot

3 tablespoons finely chopped flat-leaf parsley

2 to 3 lemons, cut into 4 wedges each

In a large bowl, whisk together the olive oil, lemon juice, oregano, salt, and pepper. Toss the fish in the marinade and let stand, covered, at room temperature for about 20 minutes.

Heat the grill to medium-hot. Lightly oil a flat, long-handled grill basket.

Place the fish, in batches, in a neat row inside the grill basket. Close the top part over the fish to secure them within. Grill, turning once, for 6 to 8 minutes, until the sardines are tender. Brush with the marinade while the fish grills. Continue with the second and third batches.

To serve the fish, spread half the onions on the bottom of a serving platter and sprinkle a little paprika over them. Place the sardines on top, and cover with the remaining onions, the parsley, and more paprika. Serve with lemon wedges on the side.

SWORDFISH SOUVLAKI
WITH LEMON-OLIVE OIL MARINADE

I HAVE MEMORIES of this dish that seem to go back forever, from Sunday outings to the Greek tavernas in Astoria, New York, when I was a child and to countless meals in seaside tavernas in Greece. You can substitute the swordfish with any firm-fleshed fish in this recipe.

MAKES 4 SERVINGS

16 bay leaves

For the marinade

1 cup extra virgin olive oil

¼ cup strained fresh lemon juice

10 pitted Greek green olives, very finely chopped

1 large garlic clove, minced

½ teaspoon grated lemon zest

Freshly ground black pepper to taste

1½ pounds skinless, boneless swordfish steaks or steaks cut from another firm-fleshed white fish, such as halibut or cod, cut into 16 equal-size cubes

Vegetable oil for brushing grill rack

16 cherry tomatoes

4 medium red onions, peeled and quartered

4 (15-inch) metal skewers

Soak the bay leaves in warm water for 1 hour to soften.

Make the marinade: In a medium bowl, whisk together the olive oil and lemon juice until blended and emulsified. Add the olives, garlic, lemon zest, and pepper and continue mixing to combine.

Place the fish and the marinade in a covered bowl or in a zippered bag and marinate at room temperature for 30 minutes to 1 hour.

Heat the grill to medium-hot. Lightly oil the grill rack.

Remove the fish from the marinade, reserving the marinade. Thread the tomatoes, fish, bay leaves, and onion pieces in that order onto skewers, filling all but the top 1½ inches or so on each skewer. Place the swordfish souvlaki on the grill and cover it, making sure the air vents are open. Grill, turning and basting with the reserved marinade, until the fish is cooked and the vegetables are lightly charred, 10 to 12 minutes. Serve immediately.

GRILLED MACKEREL WITH CARROTS, RAISINS, PINE NUTS, AND HERBS

MACKEREL, ONE of my favorite Mediterranean fish, with its smooth, unctuous flesh and its deep flavor, is an excellent fish for the grill. I have adapted this Greco-Turkish recipe for stuffed mackerel to be done on the grill. The raisins, carrot, nuts, and croutons pressed into the mackerel's cavity make this a particularly filling entrée.

MAKES 4 SERVINGS

4 large whole mackerels, about 2 pounds each, boned (best done by fishmonger)

Salt and freshly ground black pepper to taste

Vegetable oil for brushing grill basket

For the stuffing

¹⁄₃ cup golden seedless raisins

¹⁄₃ cup brandy or dry white wine

¹⁄₃ cup pine nuts

¹⁄₄ cup olive oil, plus more for brushing fish

1 large red onion, finely chopped

1 large carrot, peeled and finely diced

1 garlic clove, minced

2 cups plain croutons or ¹⁄₄-inch dried bread cubes made from stale, hard bread

¹⁄₂ cup chopped flat-leaf parsley

1 teaspoon dried thyme

Rinse and pat dry the boned fish. Season inside and out with salt and pepper and set aside, covered, in the refrigerator until ready to use.

Make the stuffing: Soak the raisins in the brandy for 30 minutes. Heat a small nonstick skillet over medium heat and toast the pine nuts, tossing continuously, until lightly golden on both sides. Remove from the pan into a plate and set aside.

Heat the grill to medium-hot. Oil a flat, long-handled grill basket. You will need to use this to keep the stuffed fish together.

In a medium nonstick skillet, heat the olive oil over medium heat and sauté the onion and carrot for about 7 minutes, stirring. Add the garlic and stir together for another minute or so. Remove and set aside.

In a large bowl, combine the onion-carrot mixture, the croutons, raisins and brandy, pine nuts, parsley, and thyme, and season with salt and pepper. Toss well.

Place one-fourth of the filling inside the cavity of each fish, pressing it gently in to be as compact as possible. Brush the surface of the fish, on both sides, with a little olive oil. Place each stuffed fish in the middle of a 14-inch-square piece of heavy-duty aluminum foil. Bring the sides up and around and fold closed securely and relatively tightly. There should be some room between the fish and the aluminum foil but it should be fairly compact. Place in the grill basket and grill the fish for about 35 minutes, turning once after about 20 minutes. Remove and serve hot.

PROVENÇAL COD BROCHETTES

IDEALLY, THIS dish should be grilled over vine wood. In the Mediterranean, it is common to use vine cuttings as fuel, and it is available in North America in specialty grocers. The wood lends a unique flavor to any food grilled over it. The recipe will work just fine, however, on any grill or barbecue.

MAKES 4 SERVINGS

Vegetable oil for brushing grill rack

2 pounds fresh cod fillets, cut into 16 (1-inch) cubes or chunks

16 cherry tomatoes, stems removed

4 (10- or 12-inch) metal skewers

²/₃ cup plain bread crumbs

Salt and white pepper to taste

¹/₂ cup extra virgin olive oil

Heat the grill to medium-hot. Position the rack about 5 inches from the heat source. Oil the grill rack.

Thread four alternating pieces each of the fish cubes and cherry tomatoes onto each skewer.

Spread the bread crumbs onto a shallow plate and season with salt and pepper, tossing to mix. Place the olive oil in a bowl and, using a 2-inch-wide pastry brush, generously brush the brochettes with oil. Roll the brochettes in the bread crumbs, pressing lightly so that they adhere all over.

Place the brochettes on the grill and grill, turning, for a total of about 8 minutes. Remove and serve.

GREEK-STYLE GRILLED OCTOPUS

WHEN I teach cooking classes to American cooks, I show them how to clean and cook an octopus. Octopus is popular in the entire Mediterranean, but it is most closely associated with the cuisine of Greece. A good grilled octopus is like a good grilled steak—it shouldn't be too soft (most restaurants boil it to death before grilling it). You should have to work a little to get at the flavor, chewing and savoring as you would a thick T-bone.

MAKES 8 APPETIZER SERVINGS

1 large, preferably fresh, octopus, about 4 pounds

$^2/_3$ cup extra virgin olive oil

3 cups dry red wine

$^1/_2$ cup red wine vinegar

2 bay leaves, cracked

15 whole peppercorns, lightly crushed

4 garlic cloves, peeled and thinly sliced

2 tablespoons fresh oregano leaves or 2 teaspoons dried, preferably Greek

With a sharp knife, cut off the hood of the octopus just below the eyes, and using a small, sharp paring knife, dislodge and discard its beak. Rinse well.

Place the octopus, olive oil, red wine, vinegar, bay leaves, peppercorns, and garlic in a large pot. Cover and heat over medium heat. When the liquid begins to boil, reduce the heat to low and simmer the octopus for 35 to 60 minutes, depending on its innate toughness and the thickness of its tentacles. It should be bright pink, tender, but al dente. Let it cool in the pot liquid. (You can do this a day or even two days ahead of time and keep the octopus refrigerated once it cools to room temperature. Just bring it back up to room temperature before grilling.)

Heat the grill to very hot.

Remove the octopus from the pot liquid and cut into 8 pieces (along the tentacles). Remove the bay leaves from the pot. Add the oregano. Pour the pot liquid into a food processor or blender and process on high until emulsified.

Place the octopus tentacles on the grill and cook for 8 to 12 minutes, turning and brushing with the marinade. Remove and serve.

GRILLED SQUID WITH SPICY ORANGE-HONEY SAUCE

GRILLED SQUID is another classic all over the Mediterranean. One of my favorite combinations of flavors is orange, honey, and vinegar, a Mediterranean version of sweet and sour.

MAKES 4 TO 6 SERVINGS

5 pounds uncleaned fresh large squid, or 2½ pounds cleaned fresh or frozen large squid (the bodies or tubes should be 5 to 6 inches long)

½ cup strained fresh orange juice

2 tablespoons balsamic vinegar

½ teaspoon cayenne pepper

Salt to taste

Vegetable oil for brushing grill rack

3 tablespoons honey

If you are using uncleaned squid, place the squid on a cutting board and remove their heads and tentacles with a sharp knife. Pull out and discard the inner cartilage from the body of each squid (it's the long white piece). Cut the tentacles off just below the eyes and remove the hard little ball inside the tentacles. Run the squid bodies under cold water, washing thoroughly and pulling off the purple membrane.

Whisk together the orange juice, vinegar, cayenne, and salt and let the squid steep in the liquid for 1 hour, covered and at room temperature.

Heat the grill to very hot. Oil the grill rack.

Remove the squid with a slotted spoon and blot dry with paper towels. Reserve the marinade and whisk in the honey.

Place the squid and tentacles on the grill. Press down with a heavy spatula for 3 to 4 minutes per side to sear the squid. Brush the marinade over the squid, grill for about 30 seconds, flip each piece with tongs, brush the other side with the marinade, and remove. Repeat until all the squid has been grilled. The tentacles need a total of about 2 minutes.

OUZO-MARINATED GRILLED SCALLOPS WITH SPINACH AND ORANGE

OUZO AND ORANGE couple really well with seafood. This Greek-inspired dish makes for a great and healthy light meal.

MAKES 4 TO 6 SERVINGS

¼ cup extra virgin olive oil

2 tablespoons strained fresh orange juice

2 tablespoons ouzo or other anise-flavored liqueur

Salt and freshly ground black pepper to taste

2 tablespoons snipped fresh dill

1 pound large sea scallops

Vegetable oil for brushing grill basket

For the spinach

2 pounds fresh spinach

½ cup extra virgin olive oil

2 tablespoons sherry or raspberry vinegar

For the mayonnaise

½ cup good-quality mayonnaise

1 tablespoon chopped scallion greens

1 teaspoon grated orange zest

Whisk together the olive oil, orange juice, ouzo, salt, pepper, and dill in a medium bowl and add the scallops. Cover and refrigerate for 30 minutes.

Heat the grill to hot. Spray a flat, long-handled grill basket with vegetable oil or brush lightly with oil.

Make the spinach: Wash and trim the spinach. Place in a steamer basket and steam until just wilted, about 5 minutes. Remove and cool. Toss with the olive oil, vinegar, and salt and pepper. Set aside.

Make the mayonnaise: Mix the mayonnaise, scallion greens, and orange zest just before grilling.

Place the scallops in the grill basket, and grill for 5 to 7 minutes, turning the basket once, until the scallops turn white.

Make a bed of wilted spinach on each plate and add the scallops. Serve the mayonnaise on the side.

GRILLED SEA SCALLOPS WITH GREEN OLIVE RELISH

ONE OF the oddest things I have ever tasted is a handful of candied olives that I bought from a store in Shanghai. How olives ended up as candy in China is too long a story to relay here. But the idea of sweetening olives is something stalwart Europeans have taken to in the last few years. Olives and raisins, olives and figs, even olives cooked as marmalade are beginning to show up in gourmet shops and in recipes all over the region. So, taking my cue from this contemporary trend, I constructed a hot-and-sweet olive relish to accompany the flavor of buttery grilled sea scallops.

MAKES 4 SERVINGS

For the relish

2 cups pitted green olives

1 long, thin, hot, fresh chili pepper or 1 teaspoon red pepper flakes

2 tablespoons finely diced orange zest

1/3 cup fresh orange juice

2/3 cup water

1/2 cup sugar

1/4 cup honey

6 whole cloves

1 small cinnamon stick, 1 1/2 to 2 inches long

Salt to taste

3 tablespoons white wine vinegar

Make the relish: Bring a medium pot of water to a rolling boil and blanch the olives for 1 minute. Remove immediately and rinse in a colander under cold water. Drain and set aside. If using a fresh chili, blanch for 30 seconds in boiling water, remove, cool slightly, peel, and seed. If using flakes, ground lightly using a mortar and pestle.

Bring another small pot of water to a rolling boil and blanch the orange zest. Remove after 1 minute. Rinse in a fine-mesh sieve under cold water. Drain and set aside. Coarsely chop the olives. Finely chop the chili.

In a medium saucepan over high heat bring the orange juice, water, sugar, honey, cloves, and cinnamon to a boil. Reduce the heat and simmer for 10 to 12 minutes, until the liquid is reduced by about half. Add the olives and chili. Season lightly with salt. Add the vinegar. Continue simmering over low heat for 5 to 8 minutes, until the mixture is thick and pulpy. Remove and set aside. (The relish may be kept in a clean jar in the refrigerator for up to 2 weeks.)

16 large sea scallops

Salt and freshly ground black pepper

Vegetable oil for brushing grill rack

4 (10-inch) metal skewers

Bring a large pot of lightly salted water to a rolling boil and blanch the scallops for 1 minute. Remove with a slotted spoon and cool. Season with salt and pepper. (You can prepare the scallops and the relish a day ahead and grill them to finish off the dish.)

Heat the grill to hot. Oil the grill rack.

Thread four scallops each onto the skewers. Grill for 2 to 3 minutes per side. Place about $\frac{1}{2}$ cup of the relish on each of four plates and serve the scallops over the relish or on the side.

GRILLED SHRIMP WITH OUZO, LEMON, PEPPER, AND CORIANDER

SIMPLE, CLEAN, CRISP flavors characterize these delicious grilled shrimp. This recipe is excellent on a buffet or for a cocktail party around the grill.

MAKES 4 SERVINGS

2 pounds large shrimp in the shell

1 teaspoon black peppercorns

½ teaspoon coriander seeds

Grated zest of 1 lemon

1 garlic clove, minced

Salt to taste

1 cup strained fresh lemon juice

½ cup ouzo or sambuca

4 (8-inch) metal skewers

Devein the shrimp but leave the shells and tails intact.

Using a mortar and pestle, crush the peppercorns, coriander seeds, lemon zest, garlic, and salt. Whisk or shake together the lemon juice, ouzo, and spice mixture. Place the shrimp in a stainless steel bowl, pour the marinade over them, toss well, cover, and refrigerate for 3 hours or up to 12 hours.

Heat the grill to very hot.

Thread four shrimp onto each skewer. Thread the shrimp through at their thickest point, near the upper part of their body. Grill for about 4 minutes on each side, or until the shells turn bright red. Remove and serve, either on the skewers or off.

GRILLED MUSSELS
WITH ROSEMARY-GARLIC OLIVE OIL

MUSSELS, SO FLESHY and sating, make for an excellent starter or main course. You can serve this dish either way, depending on how much you portion into each plate. The rosemary–garlic olive oil is a typical Mediterranean "ablution" for everything from seafood to pork.

MAKES 4 TO 6 SERVINGS

For the sauce

½ cup plus 2 tablespoons extra virgin olive oil

1 teaspoon dried rosemary

2 garlic cloves

Salt and freshly ground black pepper to taste

2 pounds large cultivated mussels in shells (about 60)

Vegetable oil or spray for oiling grill

2 lemons, halved or cut into wedges

Heat the grill to medium-hot.

Make the sauce: Heat 2 tablespoons of the olive oil over medium heat in a nonstick medium skillet and sauté the rosemary and garlic for about 30 seconds, just until the garlic starts to turn light golden brown. Add the remaining ½ cup olive oil and heat just to warm through—you do not want to "boil" the oil. Remove and season with salt and pepper. Set aside, covered, to keep warm.

Discard any mussels that are open or that have broken shells. Place the remaining mussels in a large basin filled with cold water and scrub well. Pull off and discard any beards on the mussels. Scrub the shells well. Drain off the water. Rinse again very well.

Oil the grill rack. Place the mussels on the grill. Close the lid on the grill (make sure the vents are open) and smoke the mussels for 3 to 5 minutes, or until they open. Remove and discard any mussels that have not opened. Serve the mussels in a large deep platter or in individual shallow bowls and drizzle the warm seasoned olive oil over them. Serve immediately with the lemons on the side.

GRILLED OYSTERS
WITH OLIVE OIL AND LEMON DRESSING

SMOKY GRILLED OYSTERS are delicious, and the saffron lemon-oil latholemono dressing is a complex, subtle foil to the oysters' delicate taste.

MAKES 4 TO 6 SERVINGS

For the latholemono dressing

1½ teaspoons dry mustard

¼ teaspoon saffron threads

¼ cup strained fresh lemon juice

1½ cups extra virgin Greek olive oil

Salt and white pepper to taste

2 teaspoons chopped fresh mint

2 teaspoons coriander seeds, toasted and pounded

4 teaspoons lemon zest, cut into thin ribbons

2 tablespoons finely chopped chives

24 oysters, washed thoroughly

Heat the grill to medium-hot.

Make the dressing: Spin the mustard, saffron, and lemon juice in a blender at high speed for 5 seconds. Slowly add the olive oil and blend until emulsified. Season with salt and pepper and set aside. (Makes 1¾ cups.)

Pound all the herbs and spices together in a mortar and pestle.

Place the oysters on the grill and brushing them continuously with the dressing, grill for 3 to 5 minutes. Remove, sprinkle with the herbs, and serve with the dressing.

SUGAR
'n' smoke

I love the incongruity of grilling something nature meant us to eat fresh and tradition taught us to bake or simmer. The sugars in fruit caramelize beautifully on the grill: the fruit acquires a complexity of flavor and texture that it doesn't normally have when fresh, even if a little of its raw crispness is sacrificed during the process.

Some fruits work better than others. Stone fruits, especially large, ripe, firm peaches and nectarines, cook up beautifully on the grill. Apples are great, too, and can be seasoned with all sorts of spices usually reserved for savory dishes.

Bananas are probably my all-time favorite fruit for the grill because they retain their billowy softness while acquiring the tough tasty lines that the grill imparts. I use them here in a dessert I make for my kids, with one of their favorite Mediterranean products, the chocolate-hazelnut cream called Nutella.

Mediterranean-style desserts on the grill, however, are not all about fruit. Borrowing from the tradition of grilled polenta, I use a grilled lemon pound cake as the backdrop for a light, lemony Mediterranean-inspired dessert. Ditto on the French toast theme, which here is offered as grilled sweetened bread with a fresh fruit compote.

There is a certain elegance about grilled desserts that seems lacking in most other grilled foods, perhaps because the barbecue is something we look at as the ultimate form of prosaic, easy cooking. Desserts push the art of the grill to its limits.

GRILLED SUMMER FRUIT CUPS
WITH GREEK YOGURT

THIS IS STANDARD summer fare. It takes but a few minutes to prepare and makes for an almost instant dessert. Imported Greek yogurt is now widely a available in the United States. The top brand is called Total, and it can be found in supermarkets across the country.

MAKES 6 SERVINGS

3 large, firm, ripe peaches

3 large plums

3 large nectarines

2 cups water

2 tablespoons strained fresh lemon juice

1/2 cup (1 stick) unsalted butter, melted and clarified

3 tablespoons sugar

2 cups Greek-style strained yogurt

3 tablespoons honey, preferably Greek thyme honey

Fresh mint leaves for garnish

Wash and pat dry the fruit. Cut into 1/2-inch slices. Stir the ⬚ and lemon juice together in a small bowl and toss the fruit in the acidulated water. Let soak while you prepare the grill.

Light the grill to medium.

Remove the fruit from the water, pat dry, and toss gently in a separate bowl together with the melted butter and sugar. Place the fruit on the grill and cook, turning, until the fruit acquires grill marks on both sides and caramelizes lightly, 4 to 6 minutes. Brush with any remaining butter and sugar while grilling. Remove.

Place 1/3 cup yogurt in each of six small serving bowls. Divide the fruit into six equal portions and place over the yogurt, drizzle with the honey, and garnish with fresh mint leaves. Serve immediately.

GRILLED APPLE RINGS
WITH TAHINI-HONEY WHIPPED CREAM

THIS IS A DISH inspired from the halva-stuffed baked apples that are a very traditional taverna dessert in Greece's second largest city, Thessaloniki.

MAKES 6 SERVINGS

Combine the water and lemon juice in a medium bowl and soak the apple rings in the mixture until ready to grill.

Heat the grill to medium. Oil the grill.

Remove the apples, pat dry, and toss in a separate bowl together with the melted butter, cinnamon, and sugar.

Pour the cream, tahini, and honey into the bowl of an electric mixer. With the whisk attachment, whip at medium-high speed until the cream forms gentle peaks. Remove, cover with plastic wrap, and refrigerate until ready to use.

Place the apple rings on the grill and cook, turning, for 7 to 8 minutes, or until lightly caramelized and lined with grill marks. Brush with the remaining butter mixture as you grill. Remove the apples and let cool slightly.

Serve the apples on individual plates and top with a dollop of whipped cream. Sprinkle with sesame seeds and cinnamon, garnish with mint, and serve immediately. (Alternatively, you can stack the apple rings like napoleons, with a little whipped cream between each layer. Top with a small dollop of cream, sprinkle with sesame seeds and cinnamon, garnish with mint, and serve.)

4 cups water

1 tablespoons strained fresh lemon juice

3 large Granny Smith apples, peeled, cored, and cut into $1/4$-inch rounds

3 large McIntosh apples, peeled, cored, and cut into $1/4$-inch rounds

Vegetable oil for brushing grill rack

$1/2$ cup (1 stick) unsalted butter, melted and clarified

$1/2$ teaspoon ground cinnamon

3 tablespoons sugar

$1^1/2$ cups heavy cream

2 tablespoons tahini, at room temperature

2 tablespoons honey, preferably Greek thyme, blossom, or pine honey

6 teaspoons sesame seeds, lightly toasted

Ground cinnamon for garnish

Fresh mint leaves for garnish

GRILLED ORANGES WITH VANILLA ICE CREAM

IF CREAMSICLES could be grilled, this is what one would taste like.

MAKES 4 SERVINGS

1/3 cup honey, preferably Greek thyme, pine, or blossom honey

1/4 cup fresh lemon juice

1/4 cup fresh orange juice

1 tablespoon orange blossom water

2 teaspoons finely grated orange zest

2 teaspoons finely grated lemon zest

4 large navel oranges, each peeled and cut horizontally into 4 thick rounds

Vanilla ice cream

Fresh mint leaves for garnish

In a medium bowl, whisk together the honey, lemon and orange juices, orange blossom water, and grated zests. Dip the orange rounds into the mixture, turning to coat. Cover with plastic wrap and let macerate at room temperature for 1 hour.

Heat the grill to medium.

Remove the orange rounds from the syrup and place on the grill. Cook, turning and brushing with the marinade, for 3 to 4 minutes, until caramelized and charred here and there with grill marks.

Fan out four slices of grilled orange on each of four serving plates. Top with vanilla ice cream, drizzle with the remaining syrup, and garnish with mint. Serve immediately.

GRILLED BANANA SPLIT WITH NUTELLA AND CRUMBLED NOUGAT OR GREEK PASTELLI

MAKE SURE everything that precedes this dessert is right off the grill! This is one banana split sure to send you straight to that most Mediterranean of customs, the afternoon siesta.

MAKES 4 SERVINGS

3 ounces Italian nougat or Greek pastelli

For the sauce

½ cup Nutella or other chocolate-hazelnut spread

¼ cup heavy cream

1 teaspoon almond extract

4 large, firm bananas, stem tips removed, split lengthwise, with peel on

3 tablespoons brandy or orange liqueur

2 tablespoons honey, preferably Greek thyme or pine honey

1 scant teaspoon ground cinnamon

8 scoops vanilla or chocolate ice cream

Place the nougat or pastelli on a sturdy work surface over a piece of parchment paper. Cover with another piece of parchment, and using a kitchen mallet, hammer until crumbled. Set aside. (The crushed nougat or pastelli can be made up to a week ahead and set aside in an airtight container in a cool, dry place.)

Heat the grill to medium.

Make the sauce: In a double boiler over medium heat, melt the Nutella. Add the cream and almond extract and stir until blended. Keep warm, covered with plastic and in the double boiler.

Place the bananas cut side down on the grill and cook for about 3 minutes, until the bananas are lined with grill marks. In the meantime, whisk together the brandy, honey, and cinnamon. Turn the bananas over so that the flesh side is up, brush generously with the brandy mixture, close the lid on the grill (make sure the vents are open), and continue cooking for another 2 to 3 minutes, or until the bananas are cooked through. Remove carefully.

Peel the bananas and place two grilled halves in each serving dish, preferably a glass boat. Top with two scoops of ice cream, drizzle with the sauce, and garnish with the crushed candy. Serve immediately.

GRILLED LEMON POUND CAKE
WITH PEACHES, LIMONCELLO SYRUP, AND YOGURT

INTENSELY LEMONY and fruity, this hearty dessert is lovely any time of the year. ...te other seasonal fruits besides peaches, such as nectarines, apricots, even apple slices.

...AKES 6 SERVINGS

For the peaches

2 tablespoons sugar

3 tablespoons strained fresh lemon juice

3 tablespoons unsalted butter, melted and clarified

6 large, ripe peaches, cut into $1/2$-inch slices

For the syrup

1 cup sugar

1 cup water

2 fresh mint sprigs

$1/2$ cup Limoncello (an Italian lemon-flavored liqueur)

6 whole black peppercorns

2 cups Greek- or Mediterranean-style strained yogurt

Finely grated zest of 1 lemon

2 teaspoons confectioners' sugar

6 slices good-quality lemon pound cake

6 tablespoons unsalted butter, melted and clarified

Fresh mint leaves for garnish

Prepare the peaches: Combine the sugar, lemon juice, and butter in a small bowl and toss the peaches in the mixture. Set aside, covered, until ready to use.

Make the syrup: Combine the sugar and water in a small saucepan and heat over medium-high heat. Bring to a boil, reduce the heat, add the mint sprigs, and simmer for 7 minutes. Add the Limoncello and peppercorns, bring back to a boil over high heat, reduce the heat, and simmer another 3 to 4 minutes, until the alcohol boils off and the syrup is thick. Set aside. (Makes about $1^{1}/_{2}$ cups.)

Using a wire whisk, mix the yogurt, zest, and confectioners' sugar in a medium bowl and set aside, covered and refrigerated, until ready to use.

Heat the grill to medium.

Brush the pound cake on both sides with melted butter and grill until golden and lightly lined with grill marks, about 4 minutes. Set aside. Remove the peaches from the soaking liquid with a slotted spoon and grill for 4 to 5 minutes, until lightly caramelized and lined with grill marks. While grilling, brush with the butter-sugar mixture. Remove and set aside.

Place one slice of cake on each serving plate, top with some grilled peaches, then with a little of the yogurt. Drizzle with the syrup. Garnish with mint and serve immediately.

GRILLED RICOTTA SALATA AND FRESH FIGS WITH PEPPERED OUZO SYRUP

CERTAIN CHEESES seem made for fruits, and both ricotta salata and the Greek manouri, which are similar, are among them. Both are mild but creamy and go very well with figs. The figs here are skewered and lightly caramelized on the grill, which adds a dramatic element to this otherwise simple home dessert.

MAKES 4 SERVINGS

4 (8-inch) wooden skewers

1¹/₂ cups water

¹/₂ cup sugar

¹/₂ cup honey

¹/₂ cup ouzo

8 whole black peppercorns

16 large, firm, ripe purple figs

4 (¹/₂-inch) slices ricotta salata or Greek manouri cheese

Fresh mint for garnish

Soak the skewers in a pan of cold water for 30 minutes. Remove.

In a medium saucepan, bring the water, sugar, and honey to a boil over medium-high heat, stirring until the sugar is dissolved. Add the ouzo and peppercorns. Reduce to a simmer and cook for about 10 minutes, until the syrup thickens enough to coat the back of a spoon. Remove from the heat.

Heat the grill to medium and oil the grill rack.

Carefully thread four figs on each skewer, pushing the skewer diagonally through the center of each fig. Brush with a little of the syrup and grill, turning, for 3 to 4 minutes, until lightly caramelized. Remove.

Raise the heat to medium-high if using gas or adjust the coals for more heat. Grill the cheese rounds, turning, until they just begin to acquire grill marks, about 2 minutes per side.

Place a round of cheese on each of four serving plates and place a skewer of grilled figs over it. Drizzle with the syrup, garnish with mint, and serve.

GRILLED GRAPE AND PLUM PACKETS WITH WHIPPED MASCARPONE

THIS IS easy to assemble ahead of time and grill at the very last minute. The presentation is lovely, at once elegant but also homey.

MAKES 4 SERVINGS

1 cup sweet Port or Greek
Mavrodaphne wine

$^1/_2$ cup sugar

3 whole cloves

1 small cinnamon stick,
broken in half

4 large, firm, ripe pitted plums,
cut into $^1/_3$-inch-wide slices

1 cup seedless purple grapes,
halved lengthwise

2 tablespoons unsalted butter

1 cup mascarpone

1 teaspoon finely grated
orange zest

In a small saucepan, bring the wine and sugar to a boil over medium-high heat. Reduce to a simmer, add the cloves and cinnamon stick, and continue cooking until the mixture is reduced by half and syrupy, 15 to 20 minutes. Remove and set aside to cool.

Heat the grill to medium. Cut four pieces of parchment paper into 12 × 15-inch pieces.

In a small bowl, toss the plums and grapes with 2 tablespoons of the wine syrup. Divide the mixture into four equal portions and spoon each into the center of a parchment piece. Dot each portion of fruit with $^1/_2$ tablespoon butter. Bring together the long sides of each packet and roll together to cover the fruit packets. Bring up the two ends and roll together to seal the packets. Grill the packets over a warm, not hot, part of the grill for about 12 minutes. The fruit will have softened and the syrup thickened slightly.

While the packets are grilling, whisk together the mascarpone, orange zest, and remaining syrup until smooth. To serve, place each packet on an individual serving plate, open slightly, and add one-fourth of the mascarpone mixture on top. Serve immediately.

GRILLED PAIN PERDU WITH BERRY COMPOTE AND AMARETTO ZABAGLIONE

WE EAT THIS for Sunday brunch in the summer, and make it with local wild blackberries. The bitter almond liqueur adds an unexpected dimension to the luscious berries. Top it if you like with a sprinkling of lightly toasted blanched almond slivers and a sprig of mint.

MAKES 6 SERVINGS

For the fruit compote

1 pint strawberries, hulled and halved

1 pint blueberries

1 pint raspberries

½ cup sugar

For the zabaglione

4 large egg yolks

¼ cup sugar

¼ cup amaretto or other bitter-almond liqueur

¼ cup water

½ cup heavy cream

2 tablespoons sugar

1 teaspoon ground cinnamon

6 (1-inch-thick) slices Greek tsoureki bread (see Note), challah, or brioche

6 tablespoons unsalted butter, melted and clarified

Prepare the compote: Gently toss the fruits and sugar together in a large bowl, cover with plastic wrap, and refrigerate for at least 1 hour or up to 4 hours.

Make the zabaglione: Place the egg yolks, sugar, amaretto, and water in the top of a double boiler and cook, whisking constantly, over medium heat for 12 to 15 minutes, or until the zabaglione is thick. Remove from the heat, place in an ice bath, and cool to room temperature. Either in an electric mixer with the whisk attachment or by hand with a wire whisk, whisk the cream until soft peaks form. Fold the whipped cream into the cooled zabaglione and chill, covered with plastic wrap. (You can prepare the fruit compote and chilled zabaglione several hours ahead of time.)

Heat the grill to medium-hot.

Combine the sugar and cinnamon in a small bowl. Brush both sides of each slice of bread with the melted butter and sprinkle both sides with cinnamon sugar. Grill on the least hot part of the grill, turning, until the bread turns golden and grill marks line both sides, 7 to 8 minutes total.

Place one slice of grilled pain perdu on each of six serving plates. Divide the fruit compote, and some of its juices, evenly among each serving and spoon over the zabaglione.

NOTE: Tsoureki is the fluffy Greek Easter bread, available year-round in Greek and Middle Eastern food shops.

INDEX

kebabs (*continued*)

shrimp, grilled, with ouzo, lemon, pepper, and coriander, 163

Spanish-style, with smoked sausage and shrimp, 96

swordfish souvlaki with lemon–olive oil marinade, 153

vegetable, Greek, 25

kebabs, chicken:

classic Greek, 88

marinated in cumin yogurt, 89

kebabs, lamb:

brochettes, Provençal-style, 94

quince, and onion skewers, 92

Turkish-style, 91

Turkish-style (ground), 109

lamb:

biftekia stuffed with spiced feta, Greek, 104

brochettes, Provençal-style, 94

burgers with onion juice marinade, Turkish, 105

chops, the best Greek, 116

chops, grilled, with roasted tomatoes and sheep's milk cheese, 115

chops, spicy Moroccan, 117

for classic shish kebab, 90

grilled, sandwiches, 113

kebabs, Turkish-style, 91

kebabs, Turkish-style (ground), 109

leg of, grilled butterflied, 112

and lettuce soup, Greek-inspired grilled, 48–49

patties, spicy tomato-rubbed, with pine nuts, 107

quince, and onion skewers, 92

for Turkish-style grilled meat patties, 106

langoustines, grilled, Greek-style pasta with tomato sauce and, 79

leeks and sweet potatoes, grilled, with mint, orange, and olive vinaigrette, 36

lemon(y):

marinated grilled split chicken, Greek, 132

and olive oil dressing, grilled oysters with, 165

–olive oil marinade, swordfish souvlaki with, 153

shrimp, grilled, with ouzo, pepper, coriander and, 163

lemon pound cake, grilled, with peaches, Limoncello syrup, and yogurt, 174

lettuce:

grilled chicken salad with raisins, orange, fennel and, 16

and lamb soup, Greek-inspired grilled, 48–49

mackerel, grilled, with carrots, raisins, pine nuts, and herbs, 154

mascarpone, whipped, grilled grape and plum packets with, 176

meats, 111–29

ground, 101–9

sausage and shrimp, smoked, Spanish-style kebabs with, 96

sausages and shrimp, grilled, bean salad with, 17

veal chops, rosemary, on the grill, 129

see also beef; lamb; pork

mint:

orange, and olive vinaigrette, grilled sweet potatoes and leeks with, 36

tabbouleh with grilled asparagus, pine nuts and, 13

-walnut pesto, grilled late summer squash with, 30

Moroccan grilled chicken, 133

Moroccan lamb chops, spicy, 117

mozzarella cheese:

breaded, and cherry tomato brochettes, 87

grilled panini with onions, arugula, basil, bresaola and, 67

penne with grilled eggplant, tomatoes and, 75

mushroom(s):

and garlic soup, grilled, 47

pesto-flavored, bruschetta with, 60

portobello, grilled, and onion sandwiches, 69

portobello, grilled, with parsley, garlic, and olive oil, 31

mussels, grilled, with rosemary-garlic olive oil, 164

raisin bread and haloumi
  sandwiches, grilled, with
  ouzo-fired grapes, 62
raisins:
  -fennel-carrot slaw, grilled quail
    with, 145
  grilled chicken salad with orange,
    fennel, lettuce and, 16
  grilled mackerel with carrots,
    pine nuts, herbs and, 154
  red pepper oil, cold yogurt soup
    with grilled zucchini and, 46
relish, green olive, grilled sea
  scallops with, 161–62
ricotta:
  short pasta tossed with grilled
    eggplant–tomato sauce and,
    76
ricotta salata:
  arugula salad with grilled
    pears, pistachios and, 3
  grilled, and fresh figs with
    peppered ouzo syrup, 175
Roquefort cheese:
  butter, chuletas with, 128
  grilled beef burgers with red
    peppers and, 103
  grilled chicken breasts with
    dried figs and, 139
rosemary:
  -garlic olive oil, grilled mussels
    with, 164
  veal chops on the grill, 129

Salads, 1–18
  arugula, with grilled pears,
    pistachios, and ricotta
    salata, 3

bean, with grilled shrimp and
  sausages, 17
chickpea, with grilled eggplant
  and tahini dressing, 11
chunky grilled root vegetable,
  8
fennel-carrot-raisin slaw, grilled
  quail with, 145
grilled chicken, with raisins,
  orange, fennel, and lettuce,
  16
grilled colored pepper, with
  herb-flavored olive oil, 6
grilled corn and potato, with
  purslane and cherry tomatoes, 14
grilled green bean, with
  charred tomatoes and feta
  vinaigrette, 4
grilled shrimp, pepper, and
  peach, 9
pasta and bean, with grilled
  celery, tomatoes, and olives,
  83
Spanish warm grilled vegetable, 5
tabbouleh with arugula, grilled
  onions, orange, and red
  pepper, 10
tabbouleh with grilled asparagus, mint, and pine nuts, 13
white bean, with grilled shrimp,
  zucchini, and onions, 18
sandwiches and breads, 53–71
  bruschetta, spicy feta and red
    pepper, 59
  bruschetta with pesto-flavored
    mushrooms, 60

Cypriot haloumi cheese and
  tomatoes on pita bread,
  grilled, 64
grilled chicken pita, with goat
  cheese, 70
grilled eggplant, red pepper,
  and cheese, 68
grilled eggplant, with yogurt-
  tahini-chipotle dressing, 65
haloumi and raisin bread,
  grilled, with ouzo-fired
  grapes, 62
lamb, grilled, 113
panini with onions, arugula,
  basil, mozzarella, and
  bresaola, grilled, 67
pita, grilled Greek cheese in
  pita, 71
pizza with onions, olives, and
  feta cheese, grilled Greek,
  54–55
portobello and onion, grilled,
  69
whole wheat pizza with red
  peppers, goat cheese, and
  basil, grilled, 57–58
sardines, grilled, with onion rings
  and herbs, 151
sauces:
  cinnamon-scented tomato,
    eggplant rolls with, 29
  garlicky grilled clam, spaghetti
    with, 77
  grilled eggplant–tomato, short
    pasta tossed with ricotta
    and, 76
  smoked tomato, grilled
    eggplant with yogurt and, 28